John Gower

THE MINOR LATIN WORKS

with

IN PRAISE OF PEACE

MIDDLE ENGLISH TEXTS SERIES

The Middle English Texts Series is designed for classroom use. Its goal is to make available to teachers and students texts that occupy an important place in the literary and cultural canon but have not been readily available in student editions. The series does not include those authors, such as Chaucer, Langland, or Malory, whose English works are normally in print in good student editions. The focus is, instead, upon Middle English literature adjacent to those authors that teachers need in compiling the syllabuses they wish to teach. The editions maintain the linguistic integrity of the original work but within the parameters of modern reading conventions. Middle English Texts Series includes a few adjunct texts that are in a language other than English. These texts are intimately tied to Middle English writers, their English writings, or the political and social scene in which they write. These volumes differ from the TEAMS Documents of Practice Series in that the focus is always to be literary. Sometimes the texts will be by writers who are well known for their work in English. The foreign language texts are printed with facing-page translations and include explanatory as well as textual notes. The adjunct volumes will occasionally include appendices to assist in identifying the centrality of the work to literary activities.

John Gower

THE MINOR LATIN WORKS

Edited and Translated by
R. F. Yeager

with

IN PRAISE OF PEACE
Edited by Michael Livingston

Published for TEAMS
(The Consortium for the Teaching of the Middle Ages)
in Association with the University of Rochester

by

MEDIEVAL INSTITUTE PUBLICATIONS
Kalamazoo, Michigan
2005

Library of Congress Cataloging-in-Publication Data

Gower, John, 1325?-1408.
 The minor Latin works / John Gower ; edited and translated by R.F. Yeager. With In praise of peace / edited by Michael Livingston.
     p. cm. -- (Middle English texts series)
 Includes fifteen of John Gower's minor Latin poems with facing English translations, followed by English explanatory and textual notes; In praise of peace is in its original Middle English.
 "Published for TEAMS (The Consortium for the Teaching of the Middle Ages) in association with the University of Rochester."
 Includes bibliographical references.
 ISBN 1-58044-097-5 (pbk. : alk. paper)
 1. Gower, John, 1325?-1408--Translations into English. 2. Latin poetry, Medieval and modern--Translations into English. I. Yeager, Robert F. II. Livingston, Michael, 1975- III. Gower, John, 1325?-1408. In praise of peace. IV. Title: In praise of peace. V. Title. VI. Middle English texts (Kalamazoo, Mich.)
 PA8520.G74A2 2005
 871'.04--dc22

                                                          2005030441

ISBN 1-58044-097-5

Printed in the United States of America

❧ CONTENTS

ACKNOWLEDGMENTS

Foremost among the pleasures of finishing work of any kind is the opportunity to thank those whose help was both timely and indispensable. One or another of these translations, at one or another time, has benefited greatly from the learning and good will of Brian S. Hook, Michael Kucszynski, Robert J. Meindl, and Winthrop Wetherbee. Henry Ansgar Kelly read them all, and to his extraordinary *Latinitas* and generosity of spirit this volume owes a vast debt — one I may perhaps be able to repay, only if Plato was right, sometime in life-time six or seven. I am also grateful to Emily Rebekah Huber of the Middle English Texts Series at Rochester and to Andrew S. Galloway, both of whom read the manuscript for METS and deserve credit for insightful correction and care. Michael Livingston, assistant editor of the series, expended yeoman's effort. In addition to formatting the whole of the volume, to his capable hand should be attributed the preparation of the Latin text, based on comparison of Macaulay with all known manuscripts, along with the relevant textual notes; he also prepared the edition of *In Praise of Peace*. I am indebted as well to his judicious diligence for providing an early draft of explanatory notes and introductions to the Latin poems. To David R. Carlson, *ex animo*, whose knowledge of Gower's Latin so often exceeds my own: *Ad astra per aspere, frater. Gratias ago.*

Finally, without the many extra-textual efforts and inexhaustible support of Helen Cooper, Richard Firth Green, Terry Jones, V. A. Kolve, Alastair Minnis, Derek Pearsall, Russell A. Peck, and Winthrop Wetherbee, this volume would be yet a twinkle in the eye of a much wryer time. *Amor vincit omnia, amici.* Many thanks.

We all owe thanks to Patricia Hollahan and her staff at Medieval Institute Publications for their keen diligence in reading over the volume and helping bring it to the happy state of completion.

Last, our thanks go to the National Endowment for the Humanities for continuing its vital support of the series.

MINOR LATIN WORKS

✨ INTRODUCTION

That John Gower's minor Latin poems should be among the last of his works to be trans-lated into his native English in a way is apt, since they seem to have been among the last po-etry he wrote — although assigning most of them anything but approximate dates of com-position is impossible. As the poem *Eneidos Bucolis* (attributed to a "Philosopher," but possibly by Gower himself; see Appendix 1) takes note, Gower's achievement in writing substantially in all three primary languages of his time — Anglo-French, English, and Latin — was a source of pride to others and, undoubtedly, to him too: into the final years of his life he con-tinued to produce poetry in all three languages. At the very end, however (if we can read aright the poems *Dicunt scripture* and *Orate pro anima*, seemingly written, respectively, along with his will and for display upon his tomb), his final metered thoughts were in Latin, the language that Gower, like most of his contemporaries, associated with timeless authority.

As a late medieval English Latinist Gower exhibits, in his minor poems as elsewhere, most of the traits of his time — which is to say, when compared to the great Augustan writers whose work he knew and admired (much of Ovid he seems to have got by heart), he comes at times somewhat rudely off, reliant as he was upon authorial models less classical than con-temporary. (A. G. Rigg has observed, for example, that the *Vox Clamantis* "is the first sub-stantial Anglo-Latin work in unrhymed elegiac couplets since Henry of Avranches [fl. 1220–60]" — a comment that, depending upon one's opinion of Henry of Avranches, can betoken well or ill. Rigg does, in any case, suggest the extensive range of Gower's reading.)[1] More-over, in his later years, as these shorter poems illustrate especially well, Gower initiated ex-periments with rhyme and the mixing of metrical forms within the same poem. While these clearly indicate a desire to achieve greater stylistic ornamentation, both nevertheless place demands upon his language, and occasionally force grammatical anomalies when a rhyme must be had. On the other hand, instances of the onomastic play, a earlier poetic choice which, in its way, too, favors formal panache over clarity of sense, are rarer in the minor poems than in the *Vox Clamantis*. In these shorter pieces (much to the relief of some), Gower seems intent on different techniques.

Such habits make these last poems difficult to fathom on occasion; but for this there may be other reasons as well, driven by their subject matter. The three longest — *De lucis scru-tinio*, *Carmen super multiplici viciorum pestilencia*, and *O deus immense* — are all poems of social conscience in the "Gower tradition" of voicing opinions critical of powerful institutions and individuals. These poems that we know today come from manuscripts copied after the rise of Gower's ultimate patron, Henry IV, a time when, presumably, a Lancastrian partisan such as Gower found the world to be a bit safer (or at least easier to decipher). We have no earlier

---

[1] Rigg, *History of Anglo-Latin Literature*, p. 287.

record of their transmission, or of what response Gower might have anticipated. Never, apparently, a courtier, but located across the Thames at Southwark during the years when these poems were written, Gower could conceivably take the pulse of his countrymen in greater variety than he might, had he been a Ricardian intimate like his friend Chaucer. Gower's knowledge of uncertain men and times may indeed have influenced his selection of Latin for these overtly political pieces, and that, perhaps, accounts for some of the obscure structure and language.

That said, however, it should be clearly noted that the best of these poems, and to some degree their collective range of subject altogether, can be read with more appreciation than apology. Gower's faults as a poet are his own, and have been much dwelt upon by his critics past and present, but by the same token so the legitimate strengths one finds here are also uniquely his. Certainly there is reason to know these poems for the light they shed on the intense partisanship and events of great moment surrounding the usurpation 1399–1400, and it is not difficult to anticipate that now, in translation, Gower's voice will be heard more often in historical studies.

In light of this, a brief overview of the last years of Richard II's reign might prove useful, by way of providing context for these poems. In early July 1397 the king arrested without warning his uncle, the duke of Gloucester, and the earls of Warwick and Arundel. Two months later a hastily summoned parliament, somewhat dubiously constituted in favor of the king, heard and upheld charges of treason against them, and also against Thomas Arundel, archbishop of Canterbury and brother to the earl, who attempted to intercede. The archbishop was stripped of his office in favor of Roger Walden, the royal treasurer, forced to forfeit his lands and sent into permanent exile. His brother the earl was executed; Warwick, apparently breaking into sobs during the proceedings, was spared the death penalty by Richard but sentenced to exile for life on the Isle of Man; and Gloucester, who had been shipped to Calais for safekeeping, was found "inexplicably" dead in his cell. (Testimony in 1399 later established that the duke had been smothered at Richard's order.) The lands and property of all three were claimed by the crown, only to be redistributed on the last day of the parliament session among the king's intimates as Richard, in an unprecedented display of royal power and cronyism, created a marquess and four new earldoms, and raised five earls to ducal status.

Nor was this the sum of the work of the St. Lambert's Day parliament. Gloucester, Warwick, and Arundel had all been leading members of the so-called Appellants, the body of lords who successfully forced Richard to submit to parliamentary curtailment of his authority and much to his resentment ruled, in effect, in his stead in 1387–88. The king's action against them in 1397 was widely understood to be revenge; but of greater significance politically was the repeal of laws restricting royal prerogatives passed a decade earlier by the so-called Merciless Parliament under direction of the Appellants. This was a necessary next step in restoring Richard to full power, and it was accomplished before parliament disbanded, not to meet again until January 1398 at Shrewsbury. Although there was no immediate reaction to all of this, neither amongst the commons nor the peerage (the presence of three hundred of the king's Cheshire archers surrounding the parliament hall having, perhaps, dampened spirits), a resultant subterranean unease seems to have been widespread across social classes thereafter — which unease, it has been suggested, Gower shared and was to prove a turning point in his subsequent opinion of Richard.

Over the fall and winter of 1397–98 conditions darkened considerably — even as their outcome may have seemed at first quite otherwise to the king. In addition to his attempt to reconfigure the peerage by creating new honors and breaking up old feudalities through the redistribution of lands, Richard set his sights lower, aiming to reform local civic institutions too. In moves that proved immensely unpopular among the commons, the king began replacing sheriffs around the countryside with others loyal to himself, while in many cases extending their tenure beyond the customary year's service. Appointments of a similar kind were made to the bench and to local commissions as well. But the main event of these months, which also seemed an opportunity to Richard, was a quarrel between Thomas Mowbray, newly created duke of Norfolk and Henry Bolingbroke, new duke of Hereford, son and heir to John of Gaunt and future king Henry IV, that erupted in charges and counter-charges of treason at the Shrewsbury parliament. Richard, appearing at first inclined to believe his cousin Henry, had Mowbray imprisoned; following hearings spread over several months, however, a trial by combat was decided upon, and set for Coventry in September 1398. Yet there, rather than let "justice take its course," the king halted the proceedings in a scene famously rendered by Shakespeare, banishing Mowbray for life with forfeiture of property, and Henry the same — although the period of exile was lessened almost immediately to ten years, with all lands to be held by the king in anticipation of Henry's return. As Henry had been himself an Appellant in 1387, albeit perhaps somewhat halfheartedly, and Mowbray may have had direct evidence of Richard's involvement in the death of Gloucester, the king had good reason to rejoice at their removal from the kingdom. For a brief time, with so many enemies banished and his authority appearing to grow, the world must have looked to Richard to be turning his way for good.

All his plans notwithstanding, matters began reversing themselves for the king in February 1399 with the death of John of Gaunt. Although not close to his nephew individually, Gaunt was loyal to the crown, and Richard had enjoyed his reliable support over many years. His death was a great loss, made much the worse by Richard's de facto confiscation of the duchy of Lancaster in direct contradiction of his several oaths to the absent Hereford to preserve Henry's inheritance until he should return from exile. But Richard wanted the vast Lancastrian revenues to fund his impending invasion of Ireland. He therefore altered Henry's banishment from ten years to life, assembled his army, and set sail in June for Waterford, leaving England in the care of his ineffectual uncle, the duke of York.

In France when he heard the news, Henry drew around him a small body of supporters, most of whom had gone into exile with him but with the important addition of Thomas Arundel, former archbishop of Canterbury. Arundel had his own scores to settle with Richard. Landing in England at Ravenspur at the end of June, Henry drew support first from the marcher lords, and subsequently from the nobility generally as he slowly traveled southward over several weeks, gathering strength as he went. Richard's arrogations of dynastic lands and elevation of his henchmen from 1397 worked against him: those with lands and titles feared the king's power to do the same to them. Conversely, Henry's repeated promises that his intent was solely to restore his rightful inheritance, and that he had no designs upon either the king's person or the crown, were reassuring. Richard compounded his difficulties by delaying his return to confront the threat for several weeks after learning of it; by the time he arrived in England in late July most of his home support had gone over to Henry. At the beginning of August Richard surrendered to Henry. A month later he was taken to the Tower of London to await his fate.

After Richard's surrender in August, Henry had summoned a parliament in the king's name to meet in Westminster at the end of September. Over the weeks prior to that body's gathering the intentions of Henry and his party shifted in regard to the crown. A committee was formed to study the situation, with a view toward putting Henry on the throne. The committee seems to have been issued a threefold charge: to determine what to do with Richard; to devise an effective plan to make Henry king; and, later, on the basis of the first two, to compose the text of a "challenge," or claim, to rule, which Henry could present at the upcoming parliament. Calls were issued to monasteries around the country to scour their chronicles for any item pertaining to the Plantagenet line, apparently to corroborate a rumor put about several years earlier by Lancastrian interests, to the effect that Edmund, known as Crouchback for his disfigured spine, was in fact the firstborn of Henry III, rather than Edward I. If true — as it patently was not — it would make Henry legitimate heir to the throne, through his mother. This was important because, even with Richard dead, Henry was not next in line; that place belonged to his cousin Mortimer. In the end, a plan evolved to induce Richard to resign power, thereby leaving a vacuum of leadership into which Henry could then step. At first Richard made this difficult. He agreed to cede governance to Henry, but not his anointed authority: Henry, in other words, could rule, but not be king, since in Richard's view kingship was a result of divine, not human, election.

With the parliament set to meet on 30 September, Lancastrian pressure on Richard grew until, on the twenty-ninth, he was finally coerced into signing documents of resignation. The next day the "parliament" met — actually an unaccountable gathering of compromised partisans — and responded to a reading of Richard's resignation with shouts of "Yes! Yes! Yes!" No formal vote was taken to accept it, nor was one recorded when the king was officially deposed; again, the "vote" was by acclamation, following the presentation of a lengthy collection of *gravamina*, or charges enumerating Richard's many crimes. Henry then read out the "challenge" prepared for him by his committee, which argued for his ascendancy on grounds of lineage, through Henry III; necessity (the country wanted proper governance) and the consequent will of God that he act; and the goodwill of his friends, which translated into "conquest." When he asked the multitude if it approved of his being king, the tumultuous answer was again, "Yes! Yes! Yes!" This "parliament" was then dissolved, having left not standard proceedings but rather an informal account of its activities inserted into the official rolls, known as the "Record and Process." Another body was summoned (with the same constituency) for 6 October. At this parliament, opened by Archbishop Arundel (who had regained both his ecclesiastical office and the chancellorship of the realm), Henry's kingship was acknowledged and the coronation set for 13 October. At this ceremony, largely to combat Richard's assertion that he alone could be true king affirmed by God, a special oil was used on Henry which, supposedly, had been given to Thomas à Becket by the Virgin Mary, to anoint a monarch destined to reunite the old Angevin empire.

With the coronation behind him, Henry nonetheless had still to deal with a Richard who, while powerless, yet was viewed by many to be the only sacral king. In December a plot by some of Richard's intimates and others was uncovered to slaughter Henry and his family at New Year and restore Richard to power. Although the revolt was put down, and several of the prominent ringleaders savagely punished, Henry took no further chances. Richard was removed north to the Lancastrian stronghold of Pontefract Castle, where he seems to have been starved to death in February on Henry's command. His body was then exhibited around the country, in order to demonstrate the reality of his death. Despite this, rumors of Richard's survival — even of his escape into hiding — persisted for the remainder of Henry's short reign, adding fuel to the flames of resistance that by 1402 had sprung up in Wales, in Scotland, and in England itself, where many of those who had believed and supported Henry's cause when it was merely to regain his rightful lands and title rebelled against his usurpation.

It was during these parlous times that Gower composed most of the poems included here, very probably at official urging, if not direct commission. It is likely, for example, that *O deus immense* was written in 1399, and reflects Gower's knowledge of the *gravamina* brought to bear at Richard's deposition. (Gower may, indeed, have been among the ecstatic crowd — although such behavior hardly suits his persona.) Alternatively, it has been suggested that the poem was written with Richard in mind, during the upsurge of his autocracy in 1397–98. Another case in point might be the three poems deemed the "laureate group" by John Fisher — *Rex celi deus*, *O recolende*, and *H. aquile pullus* — which (probably in that order) Gower wrote for Henry, first to gild his "election" by the crowd at Westminster on 30 September 1399, next his coronation on 13 October, and then the elevation of young Henry of Monmouth to Prince of Wales on the fifteenth (or perhaps on the twenty-third, when the prince was also made duke of Aquitaine, to commemorate both simultaneously).[2]

All are important documents historically; but they are also poems admirable equally for their skill and craft. In *Rex celi deus*, to cite a single example, Gower centonically harvests over half the lines from Book VI of the *Vox Clamantis*, a section where previously they had offered advice to Richard II. Far from the "schoolboy plagiarism" with which Gower in less thoughtful days has been charged, the practice here if recognized would seem to yield a double reward: at once presenting subtle but convincing testimony of Gower's new loyalty, while honoring Henry's accession into what was Richard's role. Nevertheless, alongside, *soto voce* and subtlest of all, comes a characteristic Gowerian warning: kings' names are as interchangeable in poems as the temptations of power to overstep itself are pitfalls encountered by rulers of every time and clime.

Similarly remarkable in its making is *De lucis scrutinio*. Its attack upon the worldliness of contemporary society is scathing, the impact rendered the greater by the extended, sinuously adaptive metaphor of light and darkness around which the poem is built. Variously meaning knowledge, proper doctrine, the life and being of Christ himself, light stands in imperiled opposition to a plague of darknesses rising from human ignorance (gestative of schism and heresies) and willingness to exceed the boundaries of law, canonical and secular. No class is exempt here, from popes and kings to knights and commons, and at first glance it has about it a familiar ring of work done elsewhere, in fuller detail, in the *Mirour de l'Omme* and the *Vox Clamantis*. Read more closely, however, with full cognizance of the extraordinarily Miltonic biblical reflections Gower includes, especially of the psalms, the power of light and dark gathers an intensity and depth unsustainable over a longer poem (except for Milton's), and fully justifies the integrity of the separate, shorter work.[3]

At 321 lines, *Carmen super multiplici viciorum pestilencia* is the longest of the minor poems, and by a great margin the one most copied in surviving manuscripts. Like *De lucis scrutinio*, its referential roots are deep in the Bible; but its central metaphor, no more the cosmic conflict of light and dark, has become concrete and corporeal — worldly sins Pride, Lust, and Avarice and heresy presented as plague upon the body (an image Gower uses in other

---

[2] Fisher, *John Gower*, p. 99.

[3] "The play upon light, sight, virtue, and their contraries" in *De lucis scrutinio* was "unbearably Miltonic" for Fisher (*John Gower*, pp. 129–30), who compares Gower's 103 lines to Milton's sonnet, "When I Consider How My Life Is Spent."

minor poems too) — so is its range of substantiating reference that much wider, embracing doctrine traceable to Boethius, Alan of Lille, John of Salisbury, and Thomas Aquinas. Not precisely Gower's shorter tour de force (for this there could be several candidates), *Carmen super multiplici viciorum pestilencia* nonetheless offers in relatively brief space a sounding of the depth and breadth of his learning. As an early reaction to the transformation of Lollard belief from the private to the public sphere, it holds significant interest as well: its occasion may well have been the nailing of the Lollard manifestoes on the doors of Westminster Hall and St. Paul's in 1395.

A word should be said, too, for the man John Gower as he emerges from the minor poems. The larger lineaments are there from acquaintance with the *Mirour, Vox, Cronica Tripertita*, and *Confessio*: the moral castigator of a lax humanity, his pious orthodoxy in politics and faith, the periodic outbreaks of prolixity, and judgments sometimes more proverbial than profound. But here are also glimpses of a different sort, a different face behind the mask. *Est amor*, thought by some to be incomplete, and *Ecce patet tensus* appear in their individual lives as stand-alone poems suddenly more suggestive of the Gower of the *Cinkante Balades* and the *Traitié* than of the *Vox Clamantis*, from which many of the lines of these two late poems are borrowed. They bespeak a softer underside, one the fierce old man found perhaps less easy to dismiss from himself in his latter years than, earlier, he did Amans' pale passion in *Confessio* VIII. *Presul ouile regis* and *H. aquile pullus* are redolent of prophecy, and show Gower the credulous, rather comic, medieval, his neck craned at the sky to see and learn the meaning of the comet of 1402, or huddled with a book of Merlin and a rumor from the street to glean the portents for his patron's benefit. Finally, in the prose and poetry of *Quicquid homo scribat, Dicunt scripture*, and *Orate pro anima* (sometimes called *Armigeri scutum*) we inherit a glimpse of Gower brought together with the "Four Last Things" that put a period to the lengthy sentence of his life, and project his imagining well beyond. That such poems should be "minor" assessed by length is no surprise: a number tell of infirmity, fatigue, the decay of strength with age at the time of their making that must needs cut all inspiration short. But in the process of translation, and the challenge to understand sufficient to supply these notes, I have often thought how richer by a degree or two we are that such bits exist, and how much lessened might we be, had their little been lost, by accident or through some deathbed authorial design.

MANUSCRIPTS

- S: Oxford, All Souls College, MS 98 [Primary base text for these poems].
- C: London, British Library, MS Cotton Tiberius A.iv.
- G: Glasgow, Hunterian Museum, MS T.2, 17.
- H: London, British Library, MS Harleian 6291.
- Tr: London, British Library, MS Additional 59495 (Trentham MS).
- B: Oxford, Bodleian Library, MS Bodley 294.
- E$_1$: San Marino, CA, Huntington Library MS Hm. 150.
- E$_2$: Ecton MS (in private hands).
- F: Oxford, Bodleian Library, MS Fairfax 3.
- H$_2$: London, British Library, MS Harleian 3869.
- H$_3$: Oxford, Bodleian Library, MS Hatton 92.
- K: Keswick Hall, MS Gurney 121.
- L: Oxford, Bodleian Library, MS Laud 719.
- L$_2$: Lincoln, Lincoln Cathedral, MS A.72.

- P₂: New York, MS Rosenbach 369.
- T₁: Dublin, Trinity College, MS D.4.
- T₂: Cambridge, Trinity College, MS 581.
- Λ: Wollaton Hall MS.

The primary source manuscript for the poems in this volume is Oxford, All Souls College MS 98 (hereafter S, according to standard denotation). Presented to archbishop of Canterbury Thomas Arundel probably in 1402, without doubt S was assembled and corrected with Gower's approval from work begun (e.g., the text of the *Vox Clamantis*) before 1399. *Rex celi deus*, *H. aquile pullus*, *O recolende*, *Carmen super multiplici viciorum pestilencia*, *De lucis scrutinio*, *Est amor*, *Quia uniusque*, *O deus immense*, *Quicquid homo scribat*, along with *Eneidos Bucolis*, possibly not by Gower, are contained in S. For versions of those poems not found in S, most (i.e., *Orate pro anima*, *Unanimes esse*, *Presul ouile Regis*, *Cultor in ecclesia*, *Dicunt scripture*) were taken from London, British Library MS Cotton Tiberius A.iv (hereafter C); for the others, manuscript sources are noted when each poem appears in the volume. All of the base texts have been checked for scribal variants (there are remarkably few) against other available sources by Michael Livingston, whose diligent notations of relevant instances are duly recorded in the Notes and gratefully acknowledged. Abbreviations in the manuscripts are silently expanded; wherever practicable, punctuation in the Latin and English translation has been aligned; and *u/v* is regularized to accord with traditional dictionary practice. Divisions in the poems, typically shown in the manuscripts with larger, rubricated initials, are here shown with bold initials, indention being used to indicated poetic structures. Other features characteristic of Gower's Latin have been left intact. The reader familiar with Classical Latin will note a number of differences between Gower's forms and those that might be expected. The following basic "rules" of Medieval Latin (though far from exhaustive) should help an initial reading of Gower's work:[4]

1. *i* and *j* are interchangeable (e.g., *reiecta* for *rejecta* — *De lucis scrutinio*, line 6).
2. *-ae-* is commonly *-e-* (e.g., *sepe* for *saepe* — *De lucis scrutinio*, line 20).
3. *-ti-* is commonly *-ci-* (e.g., *racione* for *ratione* — *De lucis scrutinio*, line 75).
4. Consonants commonly double before a short vowel (e.g., *lollia* for *lolia* — *Carmen super multiplici viciorum pestilencia*, line 20).
5. Diaeresis is commonly indicated by an added *h* (e.g., *adhibit* for *adibit* — *De lucis scrutinio*, line 102).
6. *ye-* often substitutes for *(h)ie-* (e.g., *yemps* for *hiems* — *Carmen super multiplici viciorum pestilencia*, line 187).
7. *p* commonly appears between *m* and a following consonant (e.g., *yemps* for *hiems*, above).
8. Final *-d* is unvoiced (e.g., *set* for *sed* — *De lucis scrutinio*, line 35).

In the standard edition of Gower's works, the minor poems are presented according to the order that the editor, G. C. Macaulay, found in his source manuscripts (S and C). Here whenever possible they are made to follow what can best be determined to be their order of composition, beginning with the earliest. This decision invites argument, in that it is not an easy matter in every case to date these poems. Four (*O recolende*, *Rex celi deus*, *H. aquile*

---

[4] For a more substantial outline of the differences between Classical and Medieval Latin, see *Medieval Latin*, ed. Mantello and Rigg, pp. 79–92.

pullus, Dicunt scripture) can be associated with historical events, which therefore provide at least a *terminus a quo*; five others (*Est amor, Carmen super multiplici viciorum pestilencia, O deus immense, Quicquid homo scribat, Presul ouile regis*) have headings or marginalia suggesting when they were written. Where no chronology is inferable, manuscript order is followed. Special cases are addressed individually in the Notes.

Figure 1 (facing page)

This image is one of two nearly identical illustrations of a bearded man (presumably Gower) wearing a blue coat and brown hat, with three arrows at his belt, shooting a fourth at the globe of the world. The globe is itself divided in three, each division corresponding to one of the three natural elements that make up the world: air, earth, and water. These partitions also seem to have been executed in such a way as to recall so-called T-O maps in which the whole of the world is separated geographically into three masses: Europe, Asia, and Africa. Both here and in the parallel instance in Glasgow, Hunterian Museum, MS T.2, 17, fol. 6v., the image appears at the conclusion of the list of chapters for *Vox Clamantis*; the image being followed by the actual text of that great Latin work. In both cases, too, the image is connected with a 4-line Latin poem:

> Ad mundum mitto mea iacula, dumque sagitto;
> At vbi iustus erit, nulla sagitta ferit.
> Sed male viuentes hos vulnero transgredientes;
> Conscius ergo sibi se speculetur ibi.

> "I send my darts at the world and simultaneously shoot arrows;
> But mind you, wherever there is a just man, no one will receive arrows.
> I badly wound those living in transgression, however;
> Therefore, let the thoughtful man look out for himself."

These four lines also appear in this location in the Ecton Manuscript (fol. 10r), though the image of the archer is different from those in C and G. The archer is also very different in Oxford, Bodleian Library MS Laud 719, fol. 21r, where he and the poem appear at the beginning of Book I of *Vox Clamantis*.

Figure 1: Gower Shooting an Arrow at the World.
British Library, MS Cotton Tiberius A.iv, fol. 9r.
By permission of the British Library.

1. De lucis scrutinio

Incipit tractatus "De lucis scrutinio," quam a diu viciorum tenebre, prothdolor, suffocarunt; secundum illud in evangelio, "Qui ambulat in tenebris nescit quo vadat."

☞	**H**eu, quia per crebras humus est viciata tenebras,	*(see note)*
	Vix iter humanum locus ullus habet sibi planum.	
	Si Romam pergas ut ibi tua lumina tergas,	
	Lumina mira cape, quia Rome sunt duo pape.	
5	Et si plus cleri iam debent lumina queri,	
☞	Sub modio tecta latitat lucerna reiecta.	
	Presulis officia mundus tegit absque sophia,	
	Stat sua lux nulla dum Simonis est ibi bulla;	
	Est iter hoc vile qui taliter intrat ovile,	
10	Nec bene discernit lucem qui lumina spernit.	
	Sic caput obscurum de membris nil fore purum	
	Efficit et secum sic cecus habet sibi cecum.	
☞	**A**ut si vis gressus claros, non ordo professus	*(see note)*
	Hos tibi prestabit, quos caucius umbra fugabit.	
15	Ordine claustrali manifestius in speciali	
	Lux ibi pallescit, quam mens magis invida nescit.	
	Lux et moralis tenebrescit presbiteralis:	
	Clara dies transit, nec eis lucerna remansit.	
	Sunt ibi lucerne, iocus, ocia, scorta, taberne:	
20	Quorum velamen viciis fert sepe iuvamen.	
	Sic perit exemplum lucis, quo turbida templum	
	Nebula perfudit, que lumina queque recludit.	
	Sic vice pastorum quos Cristus ab ante bonorum	
	Legerat, ecce, chorum statuit iam mundus eorum.	
☞	**S**i lux presentum scrutetur in orbe regentum,	*(see note)*
26	Horum de guerra pallet sine lumine terra.	
	Ne periant leges, iam Roma petit sibi reges,	
	Noscat ut ille pater que sit sibi credula mater.	
	Scisma modernorum patrum, novitate duorum	
30	Reges delerent, si Cristi iura viderent;	

1. AN EXAMINATION OF THE LIGHT

Here begins the tract "An Examination of the Light," which, I'm sad to say, the shadows of vice have suffocated for a long time now; just as the verse in the Gospels, "He who walks in darkness does not know where he is going."

   ☞   Alas, because the earth is defiled with dense shadows,
          There is scarcely a place that offers a level path for man's journey.
          If you go to Rome to purify your lights,
          Take marvelous lights, because there are two popes in Rome.
5   And if the lights of the clergy require more searching,
   ☞   The rejected lamp lies hidden under a bushel.
          The world hides the duties of the Church's presider far from wisdom,
          And no light shines from him while he wears the medallion of Simon;
          He takes a vile route who enters the sheepfold in such a way.
10   Nor does he well discern the light who shuns the light.
          Such a defiled head produces nothing pure from its members,
          And a man thus blind has with him one blind to himself.
   ☞   Or if you want clear steps to follow, a professed order will not show them to you,
          For shadows will obscure them with excessive caution.
15   It is especially obvious in cloistered orders
          That the light grows dim there, light which the more hateful mind does not know.
          And the moral light of priests also grows dark:
          The clear day is passing, and no lamp remains for them.
          There are lamps there, and jokes, leisure, prostitutes, taverns:
20   The veil of these things often serves as an aid for the practice of vice.
          Thus the model of light perishes, where a stormy cloud
          Has engulfed the temple, and put out all the lights.
          Thus in place of the shepherds that Christ formerly chose
          From good men, look, the world has set up a chorus.
   ☞   If the light of those now ruling the world is examined,
26   The earth grows dim because of their wars.
          Now Rome seeks kings for itself, so that the laws not be voided,
          So that that father might know which mother believes in him.
          The schism of the two new present-day fathers
30   The kings would remove, if they saw the laws of Christ;

Lux ita regalis decet ecclesiam specialis;
Qua domus alma Dei maneat sub spe requiei.
Teste paganorum bello furiente Deorum
Raro fides crescit ubi regia lux tenebrescit.
35   Hec tamen audimus, set et hec verissima scimus,
Nec capit hec mentis oculus de luce regentis.
Ulterius quere, cupias si lumen habere,
Lumina namque David sibi ceca magis titulavit.
☞   Si regni proceres aliter pro lumine queres,   *(see note)*
40   Aspice quod plenum non est ibi tempus amenum,
Dumque putas stare, palpabis iter, quia clare
Nemo videt quando veniet de turbine grando.
Divicie cece fallunt sine lumine sese;
Quam prius ille cadat, vix cernit habens ubi vadat.
45   Sic via secura procerum non est sine cura.
Stans honor ex onere sibi convenit acta videre;
Qui tamen extentum modo viderit experimentum,
De procerum spera, non surgunt lumina vera.
☞   Si bellatorum lucem scrutabor eorum,   *(see note)*
50   Lucerne lator tenebrosus adest gladiator.
Sunt ibi doctrina luxus, iactura, rapina,
Que non splendorem querunt set habere cruorem;
Et sic armatus lucem pre labe reatus
Non videt, unde status suus errat in orbe gravatus.
☞   Si lex scrutetur, ibi lux non invenietur.   *(see note)*
56   Quin, vis aut velle ius concitat esse rebelle.
Non populo lucet iudex quem Mammona ducet,
Efficit et cecum quo sepe reflectitur equm.
Ius sine iure datur, si nummus in aure loquatur;
60   Auri splendore tenebrescit lumen in ore.
Omnis legista vivit quasi lege sub ista,
Quo magis ex glosa loculi fit lex tenebrosa.
☞   Si mercatorum querantur lumina morum,   *(see note)*
Lux non fulgebit ubi fraus cum cive manebit.
65   Contegit usure subtilis forma figure
Vultum larvatum, quem diues habet similatum.
Si dolus in villa tua possit habere sigilla,
Vix reddes, clarus, bona que tibi prestat avarus;
Et sic maiores fallunt quamsepe minores,
70   Unde dolent turbe sub murmure plebis in urbe.
Sic inter cives errat sine lumine dives,
Dumque fidem nescit, lux pacis ab urbe recessit.
☞   Si patriam quero, nec ibi michi lumina spero;   *(see note)*
Nam via vulgaris tenebris viciatur amaris.
75   Plebs racione carens hec est, sine moribus, arens,
Cuius subiectam vix Cristus habet sibi sectam.

A light thus royal is especially fitting for the Church;
Under its glow the nurturing house of God may maintain its hope of peace.
The pagan gods and their raging wars bear witness that
Rarely does faith increase where the royal light grows dark.

35   We have heard these things, but we also know these things to be very true,
And the eye of our mind does not find them in the light of a present ruler.
Seek further, if you want to have light,
For David invoked lights that were more dark to him.

☞   If you look in another place at the nobility of the kingdom for light,
40   Consider that good weather is not constant there,
And while you think that it holds, you will feel your way along, for
No one sees clearly when hail will come from the whirlwind.
Blind wealth deceives itself without light;
Before any rich man falls, scarcely does he make out where he is going.

45   Thus the secure path of the nobility is not without cares.
It befits burdensome Honor to view deeds,
But nevertheless when it views the present extensive scene,
From the sphere of the nobility, true lights are not rising.

☞   If I examine the light of their warriors,
50   The gladiator is a dark bearer of light.
There one finds the teaching of wantonness, destruction, rapine,
And they do not seek splendor, but to have gore.
Thus the armed warrior, because of the stain of his sin,
Does not see the light, and his status wanders burdened in the world.

☞   If the law is examined, light will not be found there.
56   No indeed, violence and desire force law to be lawless.
No judge led by Mammon will shed any light on the people,
And, where equity is often seen, he makes it blind.
Lawless law is given if coin speaks in its ear;
60   The light in his face is dimmed by the gleam of gold.
Every lawyer lives as if under that law,
By which the law becomes darker from the word of the purse.

☞   If lights are sought in the habits of the merchants,
No light will shine out where fraud resides in the city.
65   The subtle form of usury covers the figure's
Masked face, which the rich man pretends is his own.
If deceit in your mansion could have seals,
Scarcely will you, though famous, repay the money that the miser lends you;
And thus our greater men cheat lesser men as often as they can,
70   And from this the throngs grieve, bearing the murmur of the people in the city.
Thus the rich man wanders among the citizens without light,
And since he knows no trustworthiness, the light of peace recedes in the city.

☞   If I search our country, I have no hope of finding light for myself there;
For the path of the people is corrupted by bitter darkness.
75   This is a people lacking reason, dry, without moral character,
A sect which Christ scarcely holds subject to himself.

Sunt aliqui tales quos mundus habet speciales,
Fures, raptores, homicide, turbidiores.
Sunt et conducti quidam pro munere ducti,
80   Quos facit assisa periuros luce rescisa.
Rustica ruralis non est ibi spes aliqualis,
Quo nimis obscura pallent sine lumine rura.
Sic magis illicebras mundanas quisque tenebras
Nunc petit, et vota non sunt ad lumina mota.
85   Sic prior est mundus, et si Deus esse secundus
Posset, adhuc talis foret in spe lux aliqualis.
Set quasi nunc totus Deus est a plebe remotus,
Sic absente duce perit orbis iter sine luce.
☞   **O** nimis orbatus varii de labe reatus,   *(see note)*
90   Omnis in orbe status modo stat quasi prevaricatus.
Cum tamen errantes alios, sine lege, vagantes,
Cecos deplango, mea propria viscera tango.
Cecus ut ignorat quo pergere, dumque laborat,
Sic iter explorat mea mens que flebilis orat.
95   Et quia perpendo quod lucis ad ultima tendo,
Nunc iter attendo quo perfruar in moriendo.
Tu, qui formasti lucem tenebrasque creasti,
Crimina condones et sic tua lumina dones.
In terram sero tunc quando cubicula quero,
100   Confer candelam, potero qua ferre medelam.
Hec Gower scribit lucem dum querere quibit;
     Sub spe transibit ubi gaudia lucis adhibit.
     Lucis solamen det sibi Cristus. Amen.

2. CARMEN SUPER MULTIPLICI VICIORUM PESTILENCIA

Nota consequenter carmen super multiplici viciorum pestilencia, unde tempore
Ricardi Secundi partes nostre specialius inficiebantur.

Non excusatur qui verum non fateatur,
Ut sic ponatur modus unde fides recolatur.
Qui magis ornatur sensu sua verba loquatur,
Ne lex frangatur qua Cristus sanctificatur.
5   Hoc res testatur: virtus ita nunc viciatur
Quod vix firmatur aliquis quin transgrediatur.
Hinc contristatur mea mens que sepe gravatur,
Dum contemplatur vicium quod continuatur;
Set quia speratur quod vera fides operatur,
10   Quod Deus hortatur, michi scribere penna paratur,
Ut describatur cur mundus sic variatur:
     Ecce, malignatur que modo causa datur.

> There are some men whom the world holds dear,
> Thieves, plunderers, murderers, disturbers of the peace.
> And there are witnesses, enticed by money,
80   Made perjurors by the assize cut off from light.
> There in the countryside there is no hope of any sort,
> Where the dark fields dim even more without light.
> Thus each man seeks even more the darkness of worldly seductions
> These days, and prayers are not directed towards the light.
85   Thus the world comes first, and if God could be second,
> As such there would still be some hope of light.
> But now it is as if God has totally been removed from the people,
> And, bereft of its leader, the path of the world perishes without light.
☞   **O** world so abandoned because of the stain of your manifold guilt,
90   Every class in this world now exists as if in a state of transgression.
> However when I weep for others, lost, wandering without law,
> And blind, I touch upon my own heart.
> As the blind man does not know where he goes, and on he toils,
> So my mind with tears and prayers seeks its own path.
95   And because I consider that I am headed toward the final shores of light,
> I now attend to the path by which I may achieve it when I die.
> You, who formed the light and created the darkness,
> Forgive my sins and thus grant me your light.
> Then when I seek my final resting place in the earth at last,
100   Bring me a candle, by which I can amend my way.
> **G**ower writes these things while he is able to seek the light;
> > He will pass on in hope to the place where he will come to the joys of light.
> > May Christ grant him the consolation of the light. Amen.

2. A POEM ON THE MANIFOLD PLAGUE OF VICES

Attend to the following poem on the manifold plague of vices, by which our realms
were especially infected during the reign of Richard II.

> **H**e who does not confess the truth is not excused
> From finding a way to act in good faith.
> Let the man more gifted with reason speak in his own words,
> That no law be broken by which Christ is sanctified.
5   Fact bears witness to this: virtue is now so turned to vice
> That scarcely anyone is protected from trespass.
> At this my mind is saddened and is often weighed down,
> While it contemplates the vice that is ongoing;
> But because I hope that the good faith is still efficacious,
10   What God enjoins, my pen is prepared to write,
> To describe why the world is so plague-spotted.
> > Behold, the cause that is now given is shown to be evil.

Putruerunt et corrupte sunt cicatrices a facie insipiencie, set priusquam mors ex morbo finem repente concludat, sapiencie medicinam detectis plagis cum omni diligencia sapienter investigare debemus. Unde ego, non medicus set medicine procurator, qui tanti periculi gravitatem deplangens intime contristor; quedam vulnera maiori corrupcione putrida euidenti distinccione, ut inde medicos pro salute interpellam consequenter declarare propono. Anno regni Regis Ricardi Secundi vicesimo.

pr5

Contra demonis astuciam in causa Lollardie.

      Quod patet ad limen instanti tempore crimen
      Describam primo, quo pallent alta sub ymo.
15   Nescio quid signat: plebs celica iura resignat
      Dum laicus clausas fidei vult solvere causas:
      Que Deus incepit et homo servanda recepit:
      Iam magis enervant populi quam scripta reservant,
         Unde magis clarum scribere tendo parum.
20   Lollia messis habens granum perturbat et ipsum,
         Talia qui patitur horrea sepe gravat.
      Semina perfidie sacros dispersa per agros
         Ecclesie, turbant subdola, sicque fidem.
      Inventor sceleris, sceleratus apostata primus
25   Angelicas turmas polluit ipse prius;
      Postque ruit nostros paradisi sede parentes
         Morteque vitales fecerat esse reos.
      Callidus hic serpens nec adhuc desistit in orbe,
         Quin magis in Cristi lollia messe serit.
30   Ecce novam sectam mittit, que plebis in aures
         Ad fidei dampnum scandala plura canit.
      Sic vetus insurgit heresis quasi Ioviniani,
         Unde moderna fides commaculata dolet.
      Usurpando fidem, vultum mentitur honestum
35   Caucius ut fraudem palleat inde suam.
      Sub grossa lana linum subtile tenetur,
         Simplicitas vultus corda dolosa tegit.
      Fermento veteri talis corrumpit acervum
         Qui nova conspergit et dubitanda movet;
40   Dum magis incantat, obtura tu magis aures
         Forcius et cordis ostia claude tui.
      Simplicitate tua ne credas omne quod audis;
         Que docet ambiguus auctor aborta cave.
      Nil novitatis habens tua mens fantastica cedat;
45   Ut pater ante tuus credidit, acta cole.
      Vera fides Cristi non hesitat, immo fideles
         Efficit ut credant cordis amore sui:

The wounds have rotted and been aggravated in the face of stupidity, but before the disease ends in sudden death, we ought to investigate the medicine of wisdom once we have uncovered all the injuries wisely with all diligence. Whence I, not a doctor but a dispenser of medicine, am deeply saddened in my heart, lamenting the seriousness of such great danger; and I propose to identify by clear distinction the wounds that are seriously diseased with rottenness in order to direct the doctors to cure them. In the twentieth year of King Richard.   *pr5*

Against the subtlety of the devil in the case of Lollardy.

      I will first describe the crime that appears at the threshold today
      By which the heights, subject to the Deep, grow pale.
15   I know not what it signifies: the common folk revoke Heaven's laws
      While the layman wants to reopen the settled grounds of faith.
      The written laws that God instituted and man received to be kept
      Now the peoples weaken more than follow,
          And thus I will strive to make more clear what is not clear enough.
20   The harvest with tares harms the grain itself,
          And when it suffers such things it often burdens the granaries.
      The seeds of faithfulness, scattered across the holy fields
          Of the Church, subtly deceptive, disturb it and thus the faith.
      The inventor of wickedness, that wicked first apostate,
25   Previously polluted the angelic throngs;
      And then he cast down our first parents from their seat in Paradise
          And made those children of life guilty under sentence of death.
      Nor does this sly serpent rest in the world even now,
          Rather all the more he sows tares in the harvest of Christ.
30   Behold, he sends a new sect, which into the ears of the people
         Sings many scandals to the detriment of their faith.
      Thus the old heresy arises like that of Jovinian,
         By which our stained modern faith grieves.
      In usurping the faith, it feigns an honest countenance
35   To then soften its fraud more cautiously.
      Beneath coarse wool fine linen is worn,
         Simplicity of face hides deceptive hearts.
      Such a guise corrupts the lump with old yeast,
         Scattering novelties and raising doubts.
40   The more he sings, the more you must stop up your ears
         And close more forcefully the doors of your heart.
      In your simplicity do not believe everything you hear;
         Beware the maimed doctrines that the author of ambiguity teaches.
      Your mind should hold no novelties, and let fantasies fade;
45   As your father believed before you, take up his deeds.
      The true faith of Christ does not doubt: rather,
         It makes the faithful believe in the love of their heart.

Nil valet illa fides ubi res dabit experimentum,
    Spes tamen in Cristo sola requirit eum:
50   Recta fides quicquid rectum petit, omne meretur,
    Quicquid possibile creditur, ipsa potest.
Argumenta fides dat rerum que neque sciri,
    Nec possunt verbo nec racione capi.
Subde tuam fidei mentem, quia mortis ymago
55   Iudicis eterni mistica scire nequit:
Ut solus facere voluit, sic scire volebat
    Solus, et hoc nulli participavit opus.
Una quid ad solem sintilla valet, vel ad equor
    Gutta, vel ad celum quid cinis esse potest?
60   Leticiam luctus, mors vitam, gaudia fletus
    Non norunt, nec que sunt Deitatis homo.
Non tenebre solem capiunt, non lumina cecus,
    Infima mens hominis nec capit alta Dei:
Nempe, sacri flatus archanum nobile nunquam
65   Scrutari debes, quod penetrare nequis.
Cum non sit nostrum vel mundi tempora nosse,
    Unde creaturas nosse laborat homo?
Nos sentire fidem nostra racione probatam
    Non foret humanis viribus illud opus;
70   Humanum non est opus ut transcendat ad astra,
    Quod mortalis homo non racione capit.
Ingenium tante transit virtutis in altum,
    Transcurrit superos, in Deitate manet.
Qui sapienter agit sapiat moderanter in istis;
75   Postulet ut rectam possit habere fidem:
Committat fidei quod non poterit racioni,
    Quod non dat racio, det tibi firma fides.
Quod docet ecclesia tu tantum crede, nec ultra
    Quam tibi scire datur quomodocumque stude.
80   Sufficit ut credas, est ars ubi nulla sciendi;
    Quanta potest Dominus scire nec ullus habet.
Est Deus omnipotens, et qui negat omnipotenti
    Credere posse suum denegat esse Deum.
Sic incarnatum tu debes credere Cristum
85   Virginis ex utero, qui Deus est et homo.
Vis salvus fierei? Pete, crede, stude, revereri;
    Absque magis queri, lex iubet ista geri.
Has fantasias aliter que dant heresias
    Dampnat Messias, sobrius ergo scias.
90   Tempore Ricardi, super hiis que fata tulerunt,
    Scismata Lollardi de novitate serunt:
Obstet principiis tribulos purgareque vadat
    Cultor in ecclesiis, ne rosa forte cadat.

That faith is worth nothing when experience will supply the facts,
    For hope in Christ seeks only Him:
50   Correct faith seeks whatever is correct, and merits every such thing,
    And whatever is believed to be possible, this very faith can do it.
Faith gives proofs of facts that cannot be known,
    Nor grasped, not by word nor by reasoning.
Surrender your mind to this faith, because in the image of death
55   One cannot know the mysteries of the eternal Judge:
As He alone willed to act, so He was willing to know
    Alone, and He shared this work with no one.
What does the spark add to the sun, what to the sea
    One drop, or what can an ash be against the sky?
60   Grief does not know happiness, death does not know life, joys
    Do not know tears, nor do humans know the things of God.
Shadows do not comprehend the sun, nor a blind man the light,
    And the lowly mind of man does not receive the heights of God:
For the noble mystery of the sacred breath
65   You ought never examine, because you cannot penetrate it.
Since it is not for us to know the times of the world or of ourselves,
    Why does man toil to understand creation?
To experience a faith approved by our reason
    Would not be a task for human strength;
70   It is not human to work to cross over to the stars,
    Because a mortal man cannot grasp it with his reason.
And intellect of such great power,
    It surpasses the angels, it rests in divinity.
Let the man who lives wisely moderate his knowledge in these matters;
75   Let him pray that he can have true faith;
Let him entrust to faith what he cannot entrust to reason.
    What reason does not give you, let a solid faith give.
Believe only what the Church teaches, and do not be eager
    In any way at all for what is beyond what is granted you to know.
80   It is sufficient that you believe, when there is no art of knowledge;
    No one knows such great things as the Lord can know.
God is omnipotent, and whoever says that he cannot
    Believe in His omnipotence denies that He is God.
Thus you ought to believe that Christ was born incarnate
85   From a virgin's womb, He who is God and man.
Do you want to be saved? Pray, believe, be zealous, reverent:
    Without more being asked, the Law bids such things be done.
These fantasies that otherwise produce heresies
    The Messiah condemns, therefore understand soberly.
90   In the time of Richard, concerning the things the fates have brought,
    The Lollards sow schisms of novelty:
Let the gardener obstruct their beginnings and come
    To purge the thistles in the churches, so that the rose will not die.

Contra mentis seuiciam in causa Superbie.

Deficit in verbo sensus, quo cuncta superbo
95   Scribere delicta nequeo, que sunt michi dicta.
Radix peccati fuit ille prius scelerati,
Ex quo dampnati perierunt prevaricati:
Desuper a celis deiecit eum Michaelis
Ensis ad inferni tenebras de luce superni;
100   Nec paradisus ei prebere locum requiei
Spondet ubi vere sibi gaudia posset habere.
Sic, quia deceptus alibi nequit esse receptus,
Mundum deposcit, ut in illo vivere possit.
Sic adhibendo moram venit ille superbus ad horam,
105   Quem mea mens tristis in partibus asserit istis.
Hunc ubi ponemus, hostem quem semper habemus?
Nam magis infecta veniens facit omnia tecta.
Laus ibi non lucet ubi vana superbia ducet,
Regna superborum; docet hoc vestitus eorum:
110   Cum valet ornatum sibi vanus habere paratum
Non quasi mortalis, set ut angelus evolat alis.
Militis ad formam modo pauper habet sibi normam,
Vana sit ut vestis erit inde superbia testis,
Exterius signum cor signat habere malignum,
115   Cordis et errore fortuna carebit honore.
Nos igitur talem non consociare sodalem
Expedit, ut tuti reddamur in orbe saluti.
Quod Deus odivit reprobos David hoc bene scivit,
Ipseque psalmista scripsit de talibus ista:
120   "Elatas mentes posuit de sede potentes,
Et sublimauit humiles, quos semper amavit."
Vanus non durat, quem vana superbia curat,
Hec set eum ducit ubi gracia nulla reducit.
Culpa quidem fontis latices dabit hec Acherontis,
125   Unde bibunt vani mortem quasi cotidiani.
Omne quod est natum stat ab hoc vicio viciatum,
Quo magis inmundum vir vanus habet sibi mundum.
Set qui mentali de pondere iudiciali
Istud libraret, puto quod meliora pararet.
130   Hoc nam mortale vicium stat sic generale
Quod mundum fregit, ubi singula regna subegit;
Hec etenim cedes nostras, ut dicitur, edes
Vertit, et insana dat tempora cotidiana.
O Deus eterne, culpe miserere moderne,
135   Facque pias mentes sub lege tua penitentes!
Corpus, opes, vires sapiens non sic stabilires,
Dumque superbires, subita quin sorte perires.

Against harshness of mind in matters of Pride.

Words are inadequate to describe all the failings
95   Of the proud man that have been related to me.
        Pride was the root of the sin of the first wicked person,
        On whose account those who went astray were condemned and perished:
        The sword of Michael hurled him down from the heavens
        To the darkness infernal, from the light supernal;
100   Nor did the Garden give him assurance of a place to rest
        Where he could truly have joys for himself.
        Thus, because he was deceived and could not elsewhere be received,
        He demanded the world, in order to live in it.
        By delaying, that proud one has lasted to this hour,
105   And my mind grieves to assert that he is present in these realms.
        Where will we put him, whom we hold as our constant enemy?
        For by his coming he makes all dwellings more infected.
        Praise does not shine where vain pride is at the head,
        The kingdoms of the proud; their clothing demonstrates this:
110   When the vain man esteems his apparel as having been furnished
        For him not as a mortal, but as an angel who flies with wings.
        Sometimes the poor man makes his measure the image of the soldier,
        And pride will serve as witness how vainglorious a costume can be,
        As his outward appearance signals that he has a wicked heart,
115   And by the sin of his heart his lot will lack honor.
        Therefore it serves us well not to associate with such a companion,
        That we may be restored safely to health in this world.
        David knew well that God hates those who are false,
        And the psalmist wrote these things about such men:
120   "He has cast down the lofty minds from the seats of power,
        And He has raised up the humble, whom He has always loved."
        The vain man will not endure, whom vain pride oversees,
        But his pride will lead him to a place from which no grace can return him.
        Indeed, this sin will give him the waters of the fountain of Acheron,
125   From which the vain drink death almost daily.
        Everything born has been vitiated by this vice,
        And by it the vain man pollutes his world all the more.
        But if one in his mind with a judicious weight
        Were to weigh this vice, I think he would act for the better.
130   For this mortal vice is so pervasive
        That it has shattered the world, brought kingdoms down one after another;
        It even causes our deaths, as is said, overturns our homes,
        And gives rise to seasons of madness day after day.
        O eternal God, pity our sin of these times,
135   And make our minds devout and penitent under Your law!
        Although wise, you cannot make your health, wealth, and strength so stable,
        To keep you from meeting a swift fate, as long as you are proud.

           Sunt que maiores humilis paciencia mores
           Nutrit et errores vicii facit esse minores:
140   Ergo tuam vera mentem moderare statera;
              Sit laus vel labes, pectore pondus habes.

Contra carnis lasciviam in causa Concupiscencie.

           O sexus fragilis, ex quo natura virilis
           Carnea procedit, anime que robora ledit!
           O natura viri carnalis, que stabiliri
145   Non valet, ut pura carnalia sint sibi iura!
           Federa sponsorum que sunt sacrata virorum,
           Heu! caro dissoluit, nec ibi sua debita soluit.
           Tempore presenti de carne quasi furienti,
           Turpia sunt plura, que signant dampna futura:
150   Hec desponsatis sunt metuenda satis.
           Philosophus quidam, carnis de labe remorsus,
              Plebis in exemplum talia verba refert:
           "Unam de variis penam sortitur adulter,
              Eius ut amplexus omnis in orbe luat;
155   Aut membrum perdet, aut carceris antra subibit,
              Aut cadet insanus non reputandus homo,
           Aut sibi pauperies infortunata resistet,
              Aut moriens subito transit ab orbe reus."
           Et sic luxuries fatuis sua dona refundit,
160   Vertit et econtra quicquid ab ante tulit.
           Quod prius est dulce, demonstrat finis amarum,
              Quo caro non tantum, spiritus immo cadit.
           Sic oculus cordis, carnis caligine cecus,
              Errat, et in dampnum decidit ipse suum.
165   Sic iubar humani sensus fuscatur in umbra
              Carnis, et in carnem mens racionis abit.
           Dum carnalis amor animum tenet illaqueatum,
              Sensati racio fit racionis egens;
           Stans hominis racio, calcata per omnia, carni
170   Servit, et ancille vix tenet ipsa locum.
           Non locus est in quo maneant consueta libido
              Et racio pariter; quin magis una vacat.
           Bella libido movet, favet et vecordia carnis,
              Et sua dat fedo colla premenda iugo;
175   Libera set racio mentem de morte remordet
              Carnis in obsequio, statque pudica Deo.
           Nil commune gerunt luxus sibi cum racione;
              Ista Deum retinet, illa cadaver habet:
           Sic patet ut nichil est quicquid peritura voluptas
180   Appetit in carne, que velut umbra fugit.

The character that humble patience nurtures is a greater one
And humble patience makes the errors of pride lesser:
140   Therefore balance your mind with the scales of truth,
      And keep a counterbalance in your heart, be it praise or blame.

Against the wantonness of the flesh in the case of Lust.

    O fragile sex, from which man's fleshly nature
Proceeds, which wounds his soul's strength!
O carnal nature of man, which lacks the strength
145   Of stability, so that its laws are sheer fleshliness!
The consecrated unions of spouses,
Alas! the flesh has dissolved, and does not pay its debts.
Nowadays the flesh is raging
With much foulness that bodes harm to come:
150   Married folk must be on the alert against it.
A certain philosopher, remorseful over a carnal fault,
    Gives the people this exemplum:
"The adulterer draws as his lot one punishment from many,
    So that he may atone for all his embraces in the world;
155   Either he will lose his member, or he will enter a prison cell,
    Or die insane without repute,
Or encounter poverty and ill fortune
    Or die suddenly and pass guiltily from the world."
And thus lechery pours out its gifts on the foolish,
160   Then turns and takes away whatever it gave before.
What is sweet at first proves bitter in the end,
    When not only the flesh, but even the spirit lapses.
Thus the eye of the heart, blinded by the haze of the flesh,
    Goes astray, and falls to its harm.
165   Thus the piercing light of human sense is dimmed in the shade
    Of the flesh, and the rational mind sinks into the flesh.
While fleshly love holds the mind in its webs,
    Sensible reason turns into the lack of reason;
Man's standing reason, downtrodden by everything, serves
170   The flesh, and scarcely holds its place as a handmaiden.
There is no place in which ingrained lust
    And reason can remain on equal terms without one yielding place.
Lust moves wars, and the madness of the flesh favors them,
    And bows its neck beneath the foul yoke;
175   But reason when free stings the conscience with thoughts of death
    In the service of the flesh, and reason stands chaste before God.
Lechery shares no common ground with reason:
    Reason holds on to God, lechery to a cadaver:
Thus is it clear that whatever perishable desire
180   Hungers for in the flesh is nothing, and flees like a shadow.

Pluribus exemplis tibi luxus erit fugiendus:
    Biblea que docuit, respice facta David:
Consilio Balaam luxus decepit Hebreos,
    Quos caro commaculat; carnea culpa premit.
185   Discat homo iuvenis celeri pede labitur etas,
    Nuncia dum mortis curua senecta venit:
Ecce, senilis yemps tremulo venit horrida passu,
    Et rapit a iuvene quod reparare nequit:
Vir sapiens igitur sua tempora mente revoluat,
190   Erigat et currum, quam prius inde cadat.
Heu, set in hoc vicio plebis quasi tota propago
    Carnis in obsequio stat viciata modo:
Ex causa fragili causatur fictilis etas,
    Quo nunc de facili frangitur omnis homo.
195   Carnis enim vicia sunt sic communiter acta,
    Quod de continuis vix pudet usus eis;
Cecus amor fatuos cecos sic ducit amantes,
    Quod sibi quid deceat non videt ullus amans.
Pendula res amor est, subito collapsa dolore,
200   Ordine precipiti miraque facta parat;
Sique tuam velles flammam compescere tutus,
    Artem prevideas, quam prius inde cadas.
Cum viciis aliis pugna, iubet hec tibi Paulus,
    Carnis et a bello tu fuge, solus homo;
205   Et quia vulnifico fixurus pectora telo
    Vibrat amor, caute longius inde fuge.
Vinces si fugias, vinceris sique resistas;
    Ne leo vincaris, tu lepus ergo fuge.
Mente tui cordis memorare novissima carnis.
210   Et speculo mortis respice qualis eris:
Oscula fetor erunt, amplexus vermis, et omne
    Quod fuerat placidum, pena resolvet opus.
Occupat extrema stultorum gaudia luctus,
    Et risum lacrima plena dolore madet:
215   Vana salus hominis; quam terminat egra voluptas,
    Tollit et eternum vivere vita brevis.
Crede, satis tutum tenet hoc natura statutum:
    Quo caro pollutum reddet ad yma lutum;
Cum fera mors stabit et terram terra vorabit,
220   Tunc homo gustabit quid sibi culpa dabit.
Est ubi mundicia carnis sine labe reatus,
    Casta pudicicia gaudet ad omne latus:
Stat nota bina solo quo luxus non dominatur;
    Pax manet absque dolo, longaque vita datur.

You can see from many examples that lust should be fled:
  Regard the deeds of David, which the Bible has taught:
By the counsel of Balaam wantonness deceived the Hebrews,
  Flesh stained them; fleshly guilt weighed them down.
185 Let the young man learn that life slips by at a swift pace,
  While bent old age comes as a harbinger of death:
Behold, old shaggy winter comes in with a trembling step,
  And steals from the young what they cannot regain:
Therefore let the wise man meditate on his life and times,
190 And let him direct his chariot on high, before he falls from it.
But alas, in this vice nearly the entire human race
  Now stands vitiated, in the service of the flesh:
Our age of clay is grounded on a fragile foundation,
  So that now every man is easily broken.
195 For the crimes of the flesh are so commonly committed
  That scarcely does their continuous use cause any shame:
Blind love so leads stupid blind lovers
  That no lover sees what is decent for him.
The business of love is a pendulum, now crumpled in sudden grief,
200 Now in headlong preparation it marshals miraculous deeds;
And if you want to be safe and temper the flame of your love,
  Consider the methods in advance, before you fall.
Wage war with the other vices, as Paul bids you,
  And flee from a war with the flesh, you who are only human;
205 Since love is brandishing a deadly weapon
  Fixed on your heart, be cautious, flee far away.
You will win if you flee, and you will be conquered if you resist;
  Lest you be conquered like a lion, be a hare and flee.
In the mind of your heart remember flesh's fate,
210 And regard in death's mirror what you will be:
Your kisses will be a stench, your embraces worms, and every
  Task that was pleasing will turn painful.
Mourning overtakes the final joys of fools,
  Tears of sorrow drown out laughter:
215 A man's welfare is worthless if eager pleasure ends it,
  A short life that precludes eternal life.
Take heed: nature maintains this law quite securely:
  Flesh will return its polluted clay to the earth below;
When savage death looms, and dust consumes dust,
220 Then man will taste what sin gives him.
And where there is purity of flesh without stain of guilt,
  There modest chastity rejoices on every side.
This dual distinction belongs to him alone over whom lechery holds no sway:
  Peace without deceit and a long life.

Contra mundi fallaciam in causa Periurii et Avaricie.

225   Sunt duo cognati viciorum consociati
         Orbem qui ledunt pariter, nec ab orbe recedunt:
         Iste fidem raram periurat, et alter avarum
         Causam custodit. Socios tales Deus odit.
         Primo periurum describam, postque futurum,
230   Est ubi ius rarum, scriptura remordet avaram:
         Ex vicio tali fertur origo mali.
         Nemo Dei nomen assumere debet inane,
            Falsa nec ut iuret, os perhibere malo:
         Lex vetus hoc statuit, set, prothdolor, ecce modernus
235   Munere corruptos iam novus error agit.
         Nil nisi dona videt dum se periurat Avarus,
            Eius enim sensum census ubique regit.
         Sic non liber homo librum sine pondere librat,
            Servit et ad libras quas sua libra trahit.
240   Set quia periurus defraudat iura superni,
            Iurat eum dominus iure perire suo.
         Sic lucrum siciens laqueos incurrit, et eius
            Lingua prius mendax premia mortis habet;
         Sic vendens et emens vacuus non transiet, immo
245   Munera que capiet sulphur et ignis erunt.
         Vendere iusticiam nichil est nisi vendere Cristum,
            Expectat dampnum qui facit inde forum.
         Testis erit Iudas quid erit sibi fine doloris;
            Dum crepuit medius, culpa subibat onus.
250   Penituit culpam, que semel nisi fecerat illam,
            Quod tulit et lucrum reddidit ipse statim;
          Set nec eo veniam meruit nec habere salutem;
            Iam valet exemplum tale movere virum.
         Vendidit ipse semel iustum, nos cotidianum
255   Ob lucri precium vendimus omne malum;
          Ille restauravit, set nos restringimus aurum;
            Penituit, set nos absque pavore sumus.
         Sic et avaricia, tanta feritate, perurget
            Corda viri, quod ab hoc vix homo liber abit.
260   Cessat iusticia, cessatque fides sociata,
            Fraus dolus atque suum iam subiere locum.
         Plebs sine iure manet, non est qui iura tuetur;
            Non est qui dicat, "Iura tenere decet."
         Omnibus in causis, ubi gentes commoda querunt,
265   Nunc modus est que fides non habuisse fidem.
         Vox levis illa Iacob, Esau manus hispida nuper,
            Que foret ista dies, signa futura dabant:

Against the falseness of the world in the matters of Perjury and Greed.

225   There are two vicious cousins and companions
           Who savage the world together and never leave it:
           One perjures precious truth, and the other the cause
           Of greed upholds. God hates allies of such a kind.
           First I will describe the perjurer, and afterwards,
230   Scripture with its fine law rebukes the miser,
           Saying that this vice is the origin of evil.
           No one ought to take the Lord's name in vain,
                Nor to apply his mouth to evil, in order to swear false oaths:
           The Old Law established this, but, I'm sorry to say, today
235   A new error drives men corrupted by gain.
           The greedy man sees nothing but rewards while he perjures himself,
                His census everywhere rules his sense,
           Unfree and unbalanced he balances the free man,
                And slaves for the pounds his poundage weighs down.
240   But because the perjurer defrauds the laws of the Almighty,
                The Lord swears that he will perish by his own law.
           In his thirst for profit he rushes into the snares, and
                His lying tongue will the sooner reap the rewards of death;
           Thus buying and selling he will not pass empty-handed,
245   But his rewards will be fire and brimstone.
           Selling justice is nothing other than selling Christ.
                Who does such business can expect to lose.
           Witness Judas, whose sorrow is without end;
                When his body broke in two, his guilt assumed its burden.
250   He regretted his fault as soon as he had done it,
                And the money that he took he returned immediately;
           But in so doing he did not merit forgiveness nor salvation;
                Now he serves as a warning example.
           Judas only once sold a just man; we daily
255   Sell every evil for monetary gain;
            He gave back his gold, but we hold it tighter;
                He was contrite, we feel no fear.
           This is how greed, with so much ferocity, goads
                The heart of man, so that one can scarcely be free of it.
260   Justice ceases, and the bonds of faith give way,
                And fraud and deception have now taken their place.
           The people remain without laws, and there is no one who oversees the laws;
                There is no one who says, "It is right to keep the laws."
           In all cases, where peoples seek their own advantages,
265   Our current mode is that trust is not to have had trust.
           Not long ago that smooth voice of Jacob, the hairy hand of Esau,
                Gave signs of the future, what such a day would be:

       Alterius casu stat supplantator, et eius
           Qui fuerat socius fraude subintrat opes.
270   Ex dampno fratris frater sua commoda querit;
           Unus si presit, invidet alter ei.
       Filius ante diem patruos iam spectat in annos,
           Nec videt ex oculis ceca cupido suis.
       Nunc amor est solus, nec sentit habere secundum,
275   Stans odioque tibi diligit ipse tua.
       Quid modo, cumque manus mentitur dextra sinistre,
           Dicam? Set caveat qui sapienter agit.
       Vivitur ex velle, non amplius est via tuta;
           Cuncta licent cupido, dum vacat ipse lucro.
280   Arma, rapina, dolus, amor ambiciosus habendi,
           Amplius ad proprium velle sequntur iter.
       Lex silet et nummus loquitur; ius dormit et aurum
           Pervigil insidiis vincit ubique suis.
       Hasta nocet ferri, gladius set plus nocet auri;
285   Regna terit mundi, nilque resistit ei.
       Set quia mors dubium concludit ad omnia finem,
           Est nichil hic certum preter amare Deum.
       Rebus in humanis semper quid deficit, et sic
           Ista nichil plenum fertile vita tenet.
290   Quod tibi dat proprium mundus, tibi tollit id ipsum,
           Deridensque tuum linquit inane forum.
       Quam prius in finem mundi devenerit huius,
           Nulla potest certo munere vita frui.
       Heu, quid opes opibus cumulas, qui propria queris,
295   Cum se nemo queat appropriare sibi?
       Hunc igitur mundum quia perdes, quere futurum;
           Est aliter vacuum tempus utrumque tuum.
       Mammona transibit, et avara cupido peribit,
           In cineres ibit, mors tua fata bibit.
300   Pauper ab hac vita, sic princeps, sic heremita,
           Mortuus, ad merita transiet omnis ita.
☞   Quicquid homo volvit, mors mundi cuncta revolvit,   *(see note)*
       Nemoque dissolvit quin morti debita solvit.
           Hec qui mente capit gaudia raro sapit,
305   Set sibi viventi qui consilio sapienti
       Prouidet ingenti merito placet omnipotenti.
       Tempore presenti que sunt mala proxima genti,
       Ex oculo flenti, Gower canit ista legenti:
       Quisque sue menti qui concipit aure patenti
310   Mittat, et argenti det munera largus egenti.
           Stat nam mortalis terra repleta malis.
       Hoc ego bis deno Ricardi regis in anno,
       Compaciens, animo carmen lacrimabile scribo.

The supplantor stands in the stead of another, and he wriggles
    Into the wealth of him whose partner he had been.
270   One brother seeks his profits from his brother's loss;
    If one is advanced, the other envies him.
Now a son looks to his father's years before their end,
    And blind desire does not see from its own eyes.
Now love is solitary, and desires no other:
275   It hates you, but loves what is yours.
Since the right hand lies to the left, what now
    Can I say? Let the wise man beware.
Desire now drives men's lives, and there is no longer a safe path;
    All things are permitted to the greedy man, as long as he wants for money.
280   Arms, plunder, deceit, ambitious love of gain
    More and more plot a path to their own desire.
The law is silent and money speaks; justice sleeps and ever-vigilant gold
    Is victorious everywhere with its treachery.
A spear of iron does harm, but a sword of gold does more;
285   It wears down the kingdoms of this world, and nothing can resist it.
But because death brings a doubtful end to all things,
    There is nothing certain here except loving God.
There is lack in all human affairs, and thus
    This life holds nothing full and fertile.
290   Everything worldly the world gives you it takes away.
    And mocking you it leaves your office empty.
Until it comes to its end in this world,
    No life can enjoy any sure reward.
Alas, why do you heap wealth on wealth, seeking property,
295   When no one is able to own even himself?
Therefore, since you will lose this world, seek the next;
    Otherwise the time you spend in both will be wasted.
Mammon will pass, and desire for gain will perish,
    It will proceed into the ashes, and death will drink your fate.
300   Like the pauper, so the prince, so the hermit, from this life,
    Once dead, all will pass in the same way to their rewards.
☞   Whatever man sets in motion, death unwinds everything in the world,
And no one discharges his debts without paying those he owes to death.
    Whoever understands this rarely enjoys delights,
305   But he who provides for himself while alive with wise counsel
Is deservedly pleasing to the great Almighty.
At the present time there are evils that threaten the people:
With weeping eyes, Gower sings them to his reader;
And let each reader who receives these words with open ear
310   Commit them to his mind, and let him give generously to those lacking silver.
    For the mortal earth teems with evils.
In the twentieth year of King Richard,
With compassion, I write this poem, with a woeful heart.

315

320

     Vox sonat in populo, fidei iam deficit ordo,
     Unde magis solito cessat laus debita Cristo,
     Quem peperit virgo, genitum de flamine sacro.
     Hic Deus est et homo, perfecta salus manet in quo;
     Eius ab imperio processit pacis origo,
     Que dabitur iusto paciens qui credit in ipso.
     Vir qui vult ideo pacem componere mundo:
          Pacificet primo iura tenenda Deo.

3. Est amor

Carmen quod Iohannes Gower super amoris multiplici varietate sub compendio metrice composuit.

5

10

15

     Est amor in glosa pax bellica, lis pietosa,
     Accio famosa, vaga sors, vis imperiosa,
     Pugna quietosa, victoria perniciosa,
     Regula viscosa, scola devia, lex capitosa,
     Cura molestosa, gravis ars, virtus viciosa,
     Gloria dampnosa, flens risus et ira iocosa,
     Musa dolorosa, mors leta, febris preciosa,
     Esca venenosa, fel dulce, fames animosa,
     Vitis acetosa, sitis ebria, mens furiosa,
     Flamma pruinosa, nox clara, dies tenebrosa,
     Res dedignosa, socialis et ambiciosa,
     Garrula, verbosa, secreta, silens, studiosa,
     Fabula formosa, sapiencia prestigiosa,
     Causa ruinosa, rota versa, quies operosa,
     Urticata rosa, spes stulta fidesque dolosa.

     Magnus in exiguis variatus ut est tibi clamor,
          Fixus in ambiguis motibus errat amor.
     Instruat audita tibi leccio sic repetita;
          Mors amor et vita participantur ita.

20

25

     Lex docet auctorum quod iter carnale bonorum
     Tucius est, quorum sunt federa coniugiorum,
     Fragrat ut ortorum rosa plus quam germen agrorum,
     Ordo maritorum caput est et finis amorum.
     Hec est nuptorum carnis quasi regula morum,
     Que saluandorum sacratur in orbe virorum.
     Hinc vetus annorum Gower, sub spe meritorum
     Ordine sponsorum tutus adhibo thorum.

A voice sounds among the people. The rule of fidelity gives way,
315   And praise owed to Christ is sounded less often,
Whom the Virgin bore, conceived from the Holy Breath.
He is God and man, and perfect salvation remains in Him;
From His kingdom peace began to arise,
Which will be granted to the just man who patiently believes in Him.
320   Let the man who wants to, have peace in the world in this way:
       First make peace by keeping God's laws.

3. LOVE IS

A song that John Gower composed in a few verses about the many different types
of love.

In the glossaries love is a warlike peace, a loving litigation,
Infamous lawsuit, wavering fate, unforceful force,
A peaceful fight, a ruinous victory,
A rule besmirched, an erroneous school, an irregular law,
5   A troublesome cure, a grievous art, a vicious virtue,
A damnable glory, a weeping laughter and a merry anger,
A sorrowful muse, a joyful death, a precious fever,
Poisoned food, sweet gall, life-giving hunger,
Sour grapevine, drunken thirst, furious mind,
10   A frosty flame, a bright night, a shadowy day,
A scornful condition, collegial and ambitious,
Prattling, wordy, secretive, silent, zealous,
A beautiful fiction, a juggling wisdom,
Cause catastrophic, revolving wheel, laborious rest,
15   A stinging rose, a foolish hope and a faith that lies.

Just as a great public outcry can be divided into small words,
       So love wanders in ambiguous movements but on a fixed course.
Thus a lecture heard repeatedly may instruct you:
       In this manner death, love, and life have their shares.

20   The law of the authorities teaches that the fleshly journey of good men
Is safer, when they have covenants of matrimony;
As the rose of the garden smells more fragrant than a bud of the fields,
The condition of the wedded is the beginning and the end of love.
For those married in the flesh this is like their rule of morality
25   Which makes it sacred in the world for those who are to be saved.
Thus I, Gower, old in years, in hope of favor,
Safely approach the marriage bed in the order of husbands.

4. O DEUS IMMENSE

Carmen quod Iohannes Gower, adhuc vivens, super principum regimine ultimo composuit.

O Deus immense, sub quo dominantur in ense
Quidam morosi Reges, quidam viciosi,
Disparibus meritis — sic pax, sic mocio litis.
Publica regnorum manifestant gesta suorum:
5   Quicquid delirant Reges, plectuntur Achivi;
Quo mala respirant, ubi mores sunt fugitivi.
Laus et honor Regum foret observacio legum,
Ad quas iurati sunt prima sorte vocati.
Ut celeste bonum puto concilium fore donum,
10   Quo prius in terris pax contulit oscula guerris.
Consilium dignum Regem facit esse benignum,
Est aliter signum quo spergitur omne malignum.
In bonitate pares sumat sibi consiliares
Rex bonus, et cuncta venient sibi prospera iuncta.
15   Qui regit optentum de consilio sapientum
Regnum non ledit set ab omni labe recedit;
Consilium tortum scelus omne refundit abortum
Regis in errorem, regni quo perdit amorem.
"Ve qui predaris," Ysaias clamat avaris;
20   Sic verbis claris loquitur tibi qui dominaris.
Rex qui plus aurum populi quam corda thesaurum
Computat a mente populi cadit ipse repente.
Os ubi vulgare non audet verba sonare,
Stat magis obscura sub murmure mens loqutura.
25   Que stupet in villa cicius plebs murmurat illa,
Unde malum crescit, sapiens quo sepe pavescit.
Est tibi credendum murmur satis esse timendum;
Cum sit commune, tunc te super omnia mune.
Lingua nequit fari mala, cor nec premeditari;
30   Que parat obliqus sub fraude dolosus amicus.
Mundus erit testis, vir talis ut altera pestis
Inficit occulto regnum de crimine multo.
Blandus adulator et avarus consiliator,
Quamuis non velles, plures facit esse rebelles.
35   Sepius ex herbis morbus curatur acerbis.
Sepe loquela gravis iuvat et nocet illa suavis.
Qui falsum pingunt sub fraudeque vera refingunt,
Hii sunt qui blando sermone nocent aliquando.
Rex qui conducit tales sibi scandala ducit,
40   Nomen et abducit quod nobile raro reducit.
Quod viguit mane sibi vespere transit inane,

4. O BOUNDLESS GOD

A poem that John Gower, still alive, composed concerning the most recent rule of princes.

O boundless God, under whom rule with the sword
Some moral kings, some vicious kings,
With diverse merits—now peace, now the agitation of strife—
Manifest the public deeds of their kingdoms:
5   For whatever folly the kings commit, the people are punished;
Where evils prosper, where morals are put to flight.
Observing the laws ought to be glory and distinction to kings,
To which they are sworn from the first by their allotted calling.
I consider good counsel to be a heavenly gift,
10   By which in earlier times the kiss of peace concluded the world's wars.
Worthy counsel makes a king bounteous,
In contrast to when every kind of spitefulness is spread about.
Let the good king choose counselors of similar goodness
And all things will come together for him in prosperity.
15   He who rules a kingdom that has obtained wise men's counsel
Will not damage the kingdom but will keep clear of all scandal;
Distorted counsel spreads crime of every kind in the abortive errors
Of the king, by which he loses the love of the kingdom.
"You who plunder," Isaias cries out to the avaricious;
20   Thus in clear words he speaks to you who reign.
A king who reckons gold greater than the hearts of his people
Immediately falls from the people's mind.
When the people's voice does not dare to speak out loud,
They speak their mind more darkly in murmurs.
25   Whatever is silenced in court, the commons murmur it sooner,
Whence evil increases and the wise as often pale with fear.
Believe it, a rumor suffices to raise fear
Once it becomes common, guard yourself against all things.
Tongues cannot speak nor heart premeditate the evil things
30   That a crooked devious friend deceitfully sets forth.
Let the world bear witness, such a man like another plague
Infects a kingdom with many a secret crime.
The fawning sycophant and the avaricious counselor,
However much you wish it otherwise, will cause many to rebel.
35   Often a disease is cured by bitter herbs.
Often grave speech helps and soft speech harms.
Those who paint the false with fraud give truth a new look;
They are the ones who with fawning speech at times do harm.
The king who consorts with such men brings scandal upon himself,
40   And degrades his name, which rarely recovers its nobility.
What flourishes in the morning turns worthless by evening

Dummodo creduntur que verba dolosa loquntur.
Consilio tali regnum magis in speciali
Undique turbatur, quo regis honor variatur;
45   Nunc ita, sicut heri, poterit res ista videri,
Unde magis plangit populus, quem lesio tangit.
Set premunitus non fallitur inde peritus.
Quod videt ante manum, fugit omne notabile vanum.
Cum laqueatur avis, cavet altera, sicque suavis
50   Rex pius in cura semper timet ipse futura.
Rex insensatus nullos putat esse reatus,
Quam prius ante fores casus sibi sint graviores.
Set qui prescire vult causas, expedit ire,
Plebis et audire voces per easque redire.
55   Si sit in errore regis, vel in eius honore,
Hoc de clamore populi prefertur ab ore.
Est qui morosus rex non erit ambiciosus,
Set sub eo tutum regni manet omne statutum.
Nomine preclarus nunquam fuit ullus avarus;
60   Larga manus nomen cum laude meretur et omen.
Nomen regale populi vox dat tibi; quale
Sit, bene sive male, Deus illud habet speciale.
Rex qui tutus eris, si temet noscere queris,
Ad vocem plebis aures sapienter habebis.
65   Culpe vel laudis ex plebe creatur, ut audis,
Fama ferens verba que dulcia sunt et acerba.
Fama cito crescit, subito tamen illa vanescit,
Saltem fortuna stabilis quia non manet una;
Principio scire fortunam seu stabilire,
70   Non est humanum super hoc quid ponere planum;
Fine set expertum valet omnis dicere certum,
Qualia sunt facta, quia tunc probat exitus acta.
Rex qui laudari cupit et de fine beari,
Sint sua facta bona, recoletur ut inde corona.
75   Regia precedant benefacta que crimina cedant,
Vivat ut eterno sic rex cum Rege superno.
Absque Deo vana cum sit tibi cotidiana
Pompa; recorderis, sine laude Dei morieris.
Rex sibi qui mundum prefert Cristumque secundum
80   Linquit, adherebit ubi finis laude carebit.
Regis enim vita cum sit sine laude sopita,
Nomen erat quale, dabit ultima cronica tale.
Et sic concludo breviter de carmine nudo.
Ordine quo regnant Reges, sua nomina pregnant.
85   Quo caput infirmum, nichil est de corpore firmum,
Plebs neque firmatur, ubi virtus non dominatur.
Rex qui securam laudis vult carpere curam,
Cristum preponat, Reges qui laude coronat.

By such counsel the kingdom more especially
Is disturbed on all sides, and by it the king's honor is at risk.
45   Thus presently, just as yesterday, this can be seen:
The people complain the more, whom the wound touches.
One who is prepared and expert is not deceived;
He flees whatever obvious vanity he sees before his hand.
When one bird is snared, another is wary; just so the kind
50   But dutiful king takes care always to be wary of the future.
The insensible king considers nothing to be guilt-worthy
Until matters worsen at the gates.
But whosoever wishes to know the causes, make ready to go out
And to return by listening to the voice of the people.
55   If one is with the king in error or honor,
It is made known by the cry of the people's mouth.
The king who is moral will not be ambitious,
But under him every statute of the kingdom remains safe.
The avaricious are never called admirable;
60   The generous hand deserves a name with praise and good fortune.
The voice of the people gives you the royal title; of what kind
It may be, good or evil, God takes note.
O king who will be secure, if you seek to know yourself,
You will wisely have ears for the voice of the people.
65   Rumor of blame or praise comes from the people, as you will hear,
Bearing words that are sweet and bitter.
Rumor quickly springs up and also suddenly vanishes,
Fortune is stable at least in not remaining the same.
To have foreknowledge, making Fortune stable
70   Is not human, to posit anything plainly beyond this,
But once the end is reached, everyone can speak with certainty,
The sorts of things that are done, because then the outcome proves the deeds.
The king who wishes to be praised and in the end to be blessed
Lets his deeds be good, so that his crown may be venerated.
75   Let kingly good deeds be outstanding and crimes be absent,
So that the king may dwell eternally with the King of Heaven.
Since your daily splendor would be vain without God,
Remember: you will die without God's approval.
The king who puts the world first and leaves Christ second
80   Will cling to it and at the end will feel the want of blessing.
For when a king's life ends without praise,
His name is such as to yield this kind of history.
And thus briefly I conclude this meager poem.
The kings who reign in good order, their names are fruitful.
85   When the head is infirm, nothing is firm about the body,
And the people are infirm when virtue does not rule.
The king who wants to follow a sure regimen of praise,
Let him put Christ in first place, who crowns kings with praise.

Nam qui presumit de se, cum plus sibi sumit,
90   Fine carens laude stat, fama retrograda caude.
Omni viventi scola pertinet ista regenti,
Displicet hic genti qui non placet omnipotenti;
Gracia succedit, meritis ubi culpa recedit:
Qui sic non credit, sua rex regalia ledit.
95   Non ex fatali casu set iudiciali
          Pondere regali stat medicina mali.
Plebs ut ovile gregis, mors vitaque, regula legis,
          Sub manibus regis sunt ea quanta legis.
Tanta licet pronus pro tempore det tibi thronus;
100   Sit nisi fine bonus, non honor est set onus.
Rex igitur videat cum curru quomodo vadat,
          Et sibi provideat, ne rota versa cadat.
Celorum regi pateant que scripta peregi,
          Namque sue legi res nequit ulla tegi.

5. QUIA UNUSQUISQUE

Quia unusquisque, prout a Deo accepit, aliis impartiri tenetur, Iohannes Gower super hiis que Deus sibi sensualiter donavit villicacionis sue racionem secundum aliquid alleviare cupiens, tres precipue libros per ipsum, dum vixit, doctrine causa compositos ad aliorum noticiam in lucem seriose produxit.

5   Primus liber, Gallico sermone editus, in decem dividitur partes, et tractans de viciis et virtutibus, necnon et de variss huius seculi gradibus, viam qua peccator transgressus ad sui creatoris agnicionem redire debet, recto tramite docere conatur. Titulusque libellis istius *Speculum Meditantis* nuncupatus est.

Secundus enim liber, sermone Latino metrice compositus, tractat de variss
10   infortuniis tempore regis Ricardi secundi in Anglia contingentibus: unde non solum regni proceres et communes tormenta passi sunt, set et ipse crudelissimus rex, suis ex demerites ab alto corruens, in foveam quam fecit finaliter proiectus est. Nomenque voluminis huius *Vox Clamantis* intitulatur.

Tercius vero liber, qui ob reverenciam strenuissimi domini, sui domini Henrici
15   de Lancastria, tunc Derbeie Comitis, Anglico sermone conficitur, secundum Danielis propheciam super huius mundi regnorum mutacione a tempore regis Nabugodonosor usque nunc tempora distinuit. Tractat eciam, secundum Aristotilem, super hiis quibus rex Alexander, tam in sui regimen quam aliter eius, disciplina edoctus fuit. Principalis tamen huius operis materia super amorem et infatuatas
20   amantum passiones fundamentum habet: nomenque sibi appropriatum *Confessio Amantis* specialiter sortitus est.

For he who presumes about himself, takes more to himself,

90   Ends without praise, his fame turned on its tail.

That school relates to all living rulers;

He who does not please the Almighty displeases his people.

Grace follows upon merits where blame recedes;

The king who does not believe this harms his kingly state

95   The remedy for evil consists not of fateful decree

But of judicial decree with royal gravity.

The common people like sheep in a fold, death and life, the rule of law,

In the hands of the king they are as great as you read.

May the throne bestow such great things upon you despite its temporary decline;

100   Unless it is good in the end it, it is no honor but a burden.

Therefore let the king see how he travels in his chariot,

And take care lest he lose a wheel and suffer a fall.

May what I have written be open to the King of Heaven,

For there is nothing that can be hidden from His law.

5. BECAUSE EACH ONE

1–4   Because each one is obliged to impart to others what he has received from God, John Gower, desiring to relieve to some extent the accounting of his stewardship over the things that God has given him in the flesh, with set purpose brought forth into light three books especially composed by him during his lifetime for the purpose of bringing instruction to the attention of others.

5–8   The first book, written in the French tongue, is divided into ten parts. It deals with vices and virtues and the various conditions of the world, and sets out to point the way in the direct route by which the trespassing sinner should return to his proper acknowledgement of the Creator. And the book is entitled with the name of *The Mirror of Meditation*.

9–13   The second book, composed in Latin verse, deals with the various misfortunes that occurred in England during the reign of King Richard II, when not only were tribulations suffered by the magnates and commons of the realm, but also the cruel king himself, falling from on high because of his own misdeeds, was finally cast into the ditch that he had dug. And the volume is entitled with the name of *The Voice of One Crying*.

14–21   Now the third book, written in English in honor of his valiant lord, Lord Henry of Lancaster, at the time Earl of Derby, sets out the ages according to the prophecy of Daniel concerning the changes of the kingdoms of the world from the time of King Nabuchodonosor until the present. It also deals with matters that King Alexander was instructed upon according to Aristotle, by Aristotle's own teaching, concerning his own regime and otherwise. But the principal matter of this book rests upon love and the infatuated emotions of lovers, and it has received as its appropriate name *The Lover's Confession*.

6. ECCE PATET TENSUS

Ecce, patet tensus ceci Cupidinis arcus;
    Unde sagitta volans ardor amoris erit.
Omnia vincit amor; cecus tamen errat ubique,
    Quo sibi directum carpere nescit iter.
5   Ille suos famulos ita cecos ducit amantes.
    Quod sibi quid deceat non videt ullus amans.
Sic oculus cordis carnis caligine cecus
    Decidit, et racio nil racionis habet.
Sic amor ex velle vivit, quem ceca voluptas
10   Nutrit, et ad placitum cunta ministrat ei;
Subque suis alis mundus requiescit in umbra,
    Et sua precepta quisquis ubique facit.
Ipse coronatus inopes simul atque potentes
    Omnes lege pari conficit esse pares.
15   Sic amor omne domat, quicquid natura creavit,
    Et tamen indomitus ipse per omne manet:
Carcerat et redimit, ligat atque ligata resoluit,
    Vulnerat omne genus, nec sibi vulnus habet.
Non manet in terris qui prelia vincit amoris,
20   Nec sibi quis firme federa pacis habet.
Sampsonis vires, gladius neque David — in istis
    Quid laudis — sensus aut Salomonis habent.
O natura viri, poterit quam tollere nemo,
    Nec tamen excusat quod facit ipsa malum!
25   O natura viri, que naturatur eodem
    Quod vitare nequit nec licet illud agi!
O natura viri, duo que contraria mixta
    Continet, amborum nec licet acta sequi!
O natura viri, que semper habet sibi bellum
30   Corporis ac anime, que sua iura petunt!
Sic magis igne suo Cupido perurit amantum
    Et, quasi de bello corda, subacta tenet.
Qui vult ergo sue carnis compescere flammam,
    Arcum prevideat unde sagitta volat.
35   Nullus ab innato valet hoc euadere morbo,
    Sit nisi quod sola gracia curet eum . . .

6. LO, THE TAUT BOW

Lo, here is the taut bow of the blind Cupid,
    From which the flying arrow is the flame of Love.
Love conquers all, but, being blind he strays to all places
    And knows not whither his trail will lead.
5   Thus does he lead lovers, his blind servants.
    No lover sees what is fitting for him;
Thus their eye, blinded by the fleshly heart,
    Yields, and their reason has nothing of reason about it.
Thus Love lives on will, and blind desire fosters it,
10   And bestows everything on him at his whim,
And under the shadow of his wings the world lies at rest.
    And everyone obeys his precepts.
He is the crowned king who makes all,
    Poor and powerful alike, to be equals under an equal law.
15   Thus Love subdues everything that Nature has created
    While he himself remains unsubdued by all.
He imprisons and sets free, binds and releases the bound,
    He wounds every nation, but receives no wound himself.
In the wars of Love there is no victor on earth,
20   Nor has anyone concluded with him a firm treaty of peace.
The strength of Samson and the sword of David
    Have nothing praiseworthy in them, nor the intelligence of Solomon.
O human nature, which no one can abolish,
    Nor yet excuse the evils it does!
25   O human nature, irresistibly disposed
    To that unlawful thing which it cannot shun!
O human nature, that contains two mixed contraries
    But is not allowed to follow the deeds of both!
O human nature, which always has war within itself
30   Of body and soul, both seeking the same authority!
Thus all the more Cupid assaults the hearts of lovers with his fire,
    And holds them subject as if defeated in war.
Therefore, whoever wishes to hold in check the fire of his flesh
    Let him look out for the bow from which the arrow flies.
35   No one is strong enough to evade this inborn malady,
    Unless grace provides a cure . . .

7. REX CELI DEUS

Sequitur carmen unde magnificus rex noster Henricus prenotatus apud Deum et homines cum omni benediccione glorificetur.

Rex celi, Deus et dominus, qui tempora solus
    Condidit, et solus condita cuncta regit,
Qui rerum causas ex se produxit, et unum
    In se principium rebus inesse dedit,
5   Qui dedit ut stabili motu consisteret orbis
    Fixus in eternum mobilitate sua,
Quique potens verbi produxit ad esse creata,
    Quique sue mentis lege ligavit ea,
Ipse caput regum, reges quo rectificantur,
10   Teque tuum regnum, Rex pie, queso regat.
Grata superveniens te misit gracia nobis;
    O sine labe salus nulla per ante fuit;
Sic tuus adventus nova gaudia sponte reduxit,
    Quo prius in luctu lacrima maior erat.
15   Nos tua milicia pavidos relevavit ab ymo,
    Quos prius oppressit ponderis omne malum:
Ex probitate tua, quo mors latitabat in umbra,
    Vita resurrexit clara que regna regit.
Sic tua sors sortem mediante Deo renovatam
20   Sanat et emendat, que prius egra fuit.
O pie rex, Cristum per te laudamus, et ipsum
    Qui tibi nos tribuit terra reviva colit;
Sancta sit illa dies qua tu tibi regna petisti,
    Sanctus et ille Deus, qui tibi regna dedit!
25   Qui tibi prima tulit confirmet regna futura,
    Quo poteris magno magnus honore frui:
Sit tibi progenies ita multiplicata per evum,
    Quod genus inde pium repleat omne solum;
Quicquid in orbe boni fuerit tibi summus ab alto
30   Donet, ut in terris rex in honore regas.
Omne quod est turpe vacuum discedat, et omne
    Est quod honorificum det Deus esse tuum.
Consilium nullum pie rex te tangat iniquum,
    In quibus occultum scit Deus esse dolum.
35   Absit avaricia, ne tangat regia corda,
    Nec queat in terra proditor esse tua.
Sic tua processus habeat fortuna perhennes,
    Quo recolant laudes secula cuncta tuas;
Nuper ut Augusti fuerant preconia Rome;
40   Concinat in gestis Anglia leta tuis.

7. KING OF HEAVEN

Here follows a poem by which our magnificent King Henry, singled out by God
and men with every blessing, will be glorified.

King of Heaven, God and master, who alone
    Created Time, and alone rules all created things,
Who from Himself produced the causes of things,
    And set a single principle in Himself to inhere in things,
5   Who set the world to remain with a stable movement,
    Fixed forever in its motion,
And who, powerful in word, brought all creation into being
    And who bound them by the law of His mind,
He, the head of kings, by whom kings are justified,
10   I pray that He rule you, pious king, and your kingdom.
Gratifying, supervening grace sent you to us;
    O, before that there was no safety without disaster.
Thus your coming spontaneously brought back new joys,
    Where before there had been mourning and much weeping.
15   We were cowering, and your knighthood raised us from the depths,
    Who were before oppressed by the weight of every evil:
Because of your worthiness, when death lurked in the shadows,
    The noble life that rules kingdoms arose once more.
Thus your fortune renews and heals ours, with God's help,
20   Making whole what was ailing.
O pious king, we praise Christ through you, and Him
    A revived land worships, who gave us to you.
Blessed be that day when you sought the kingship for yourself,
    And blessed be God who gave you the rule!
25   May He who gave you your first rule confirm your future rule,
    By whom you are great, and able to enjoy great honor:
May your offspring be so multiplied forever
    And may their devout race replenish all the land.
May God on high give to you all the good in the world,
30   So that you may rule as king on earth in honor.
May all that is evil disperse harmlessly, and all
    That is honorable may God grant to be yours.
Let no iniquitous counsel touch you, dutiful king,
    In things where God knows evil is hidden.
35   Let avarice be banished, let it not touch your royal heart,
    Nor allow it to be a traitor in your land.
Thus may your fortune prosper perpetually,
    So that all generations will renew your praise;
As the public criers did of old for Augustus in Rome,
40   Let a joyful England sing your deeds in one voice.

O tibi, rex, evo detur, fortissime, nostro
    Semper honorata sceptra tenere manu:
Stes ita magnanimus, quod ubi tua regna gubernas,
    Terreat has partes hostica nulla manus;
45   Augeat imperium tibi Cristus et augeat annos,
    Protegat et nostras aucta corona fores;
Sit tibi pax finis; domito domineris in orbe,
    Cunctaque sint humeris inferiora tuis:
Sic honor et virtus, laus, gloria, pax que potestas —
50   Te que tuum regnum magnificare queant.
Cordis amore tibi, pie rex, mea vota paravi;
    Est quia servicii nil nisi velle michi:
Ergo tue laudi que tuo genuflexus honori
    Verba loco doni pauper habenda tuli.
55   Est tamen ista mei, pie rex, sentencia verbi
    Fine tui regni sint tibi regna poli!

8. O RECOLENDE

Epistola brevis, unde virtutes regie morales ad sanum regimen ampliori memoria dirigantur.

O recolende, bone, pie rex, Henrice, patrone,
Ad bona dispone quos eripis a Pharaone.
Noxia depone, quibus est humus hec in agone,
Regni persone quo vivant sub racione.
5   Pacem compone, vires moderare corone,
Legibus impone frenum sine condicione,
Firmaque sermone iura tenere mone.
Rex confirmatus, licet undique magnificatus,
Sub Cristo gratus vivas tamen inmaculatus.
10   Est tibi prelatus, comes et baro, villa, Senatus,
Miles et armatus sub lege tua moderatus.
Dirige quosque status, maneas quo pacificatus;
Invidus, elatus nec avarus erit sociatus;
Sic eris ornatus, purus, ad omne latus.
15   Hec, ut amans quibit Gower, pie rex, tibi scribit:
Quo pietas ibit, ibi gracia nulla peribit;
Qui bene describit semet mala nulla subibit,
Set pius exibit, que Dei pietate redibit.
Sic qui transibit opus et pietatis adibit,
20   Hunc Deus ascribit: quod ab hoste perire nequibit;
Et sic finibit qui pia vota bibit.
Quanto regalis honor est tibi plus generalis,
Tanto moralis virtus tibi sit specialis.

O to you, most powerful king, may it be granted in our age
    That you hold the honored scepter always in your hand:
May you stand thus magnanimous, so that where you govern your kingdom
    No enemy hand may strike fear in these lands;
45   May Christ increase your empire and your years,
    And may He protect our gates with your magnified crown;
May your end be in peace, may you dominate a dominated world,
    And may all things fall beneath your sway:
Thus may honor and strength, praise, glory, peace and might
50   Have power to make you and your kingdom great.
I have formed my prayers for you with a loving heart, pious king;
    For I have no desire, save only service:
Therefore on bended knee for your praise and honor
    I a poor man instead of a gift have offered these words for you to keep.
55   But this, pious king, is the sum of my words:
    At the end of your reign, may the kingdom of heaven be yours!

8. O Venerable

A brief letter, in which the moral virtues worthy of a king for healthy governance
will be laid out, the better to keep in memory.

O venerable, good and pious King Henry, our patron,
Set up for good things those whom you rescue from Pharaoh.
Remove from them what is harmful, for whom this land is in conflict,
So that the people of the realm may live under the rule of reason.
5   Establish peace, moderate the powers of the crown,
Bridle the laws unconditionally,
Confirm rights by your command, admonish your people to keep them.
Although you are confirmed king and glorified on all sides,
Still you must live pleasing to Christ without blemish.
10   Restrained is prelate, earl and baron, city, senate,
Knight and man-at-arms under your law.
Govern every class so that you maintain a state of peace.
The envious will not be your companion, nor the avaricious;
And so you will be adorned and pure on every side.
15   **T**hese things, pious king, Gower writes to you as one who loves you:
Where mercy will go, there no grace will perish;
He who describes himself well will undergo no evil,
But will pass away proudly and return to the mercy of God.
Thus, one who passes through this life and approaches the work of mercy
20   God marks him; which can be undone by no enemy;
Thus will he end who drinks in the deeds of mercy.
The more abounding your royal honor is,
The more should moral virtue be made your own.

> Sit tibi carnalis in mundo regula qualis
> 25   Est tibi mentalis in Cristo spiritualis.
> Si fueris talis, tua cronica perpetualis
> Tunc erit equalis perfectaque materialis.
>   Rex inmortalis te regat absque malis!

9. H. AQUILE PULLUS

> **H**. aquile pullus, quo nunquam gracior ullus,
> Hostes confregit, que tirannica colla subegit.
> H. aquile cepit oleum, quo regna recepit;
> Sic veteri iuncta stipiti nova stirps redit uncta.

10. QUICQUID HOMO SCRIBAT (IN FINE)

[Trentham version]

> **H**enrici quarti primus regni fuit annus
>   Quo michi defecit visus ad acta mea.
> Omnia tempus habent; finem natura ministrat,
>   Quem virtute sua frangere nemo potest.
> 5   Ultra posse nichil, quamvis michi velle remansit;
>   Amplius ut scribam non michi posse manet.
> Dum potui scripsi, set nunc quia curua senectus
>   Turbavit sensus, scripta relinquo scolis.
> Scribat qui veniet post me discrecior alter,
> 10   Ammodo namque manus et mea penna silent.
> Hoc tamen, in fine verborum queso meorum,
>   Prospera quod statuat regna futura Deus. Amen.

[Cotton, Harleian, Glasgow version]

Nota hic in fine qualiter a principio illius cronice que *Vox Clamantis* dicitur, una cum sequenti cronica que *Tripertita* est, tam de tempore regis Ricardi secundi usque in ipsius deposicionem, quam de coronacione illustrissimi domini regis Henrici quarti usque in annum regni sui secundum, ego licet indignus inter alios scribentes scriptor a diu solicitus, precipue super hiis que medio tempore in   *pr5* Anglia contingebant, secundum varias rerum accidencias varia carmina, que ad legendum necessaria sunt, sub compendio breviter conscripsi. Et nunc, quia tam gravitate senectutis quam aliarum infirmitatum multipliciter depressus, ulterius de cronicis scribere discrete non sufficio; excusacionem meam necessariam, prout patet, consequenter declarare intendo.   *pr10*

Let the rule of fleshly life in the world be such to you
25   As is the spiritual rule of Christ in your mind.
      If you are such, your lasting record
      Will then match it and be perfect in substance.
            Let the Immortal King guide you free from evil!

9. H. SON OF THE EAGLE

H. son of the eagle, than whom no one is ever more graceful,
Has broken his enemies, and subjugated tyrannical necks.
H. the eagle has captured the oil, by which he has received the rule of the realm;
Thus the new stock returns, anointed and joined to the old stem.

10. TO WHATEVER A MAN WRITES

[Trentham version]

It was in the first year of the reign of King Henry IV
      When my sight failed for my deeds.
    All things have their time; nature applies a limit,
      Which no man can break by his own power.
5   I can do nothing beyond what is possible, though my will has remained;
      My ability to write more has not stayed.
    While I was able I wrote, but now because stooped old age
      Has troubled my senses, I leave writing to the schools.
    Let someone else more discreet who comes after me write,
10   For from this time forth my hand and pen will be silent.
    Nevertheless I ask this one final thing, the last of my words:
      That God make our kingdoms prosperous in the future. Amen.

[Cotton, Harleian, Glasgow version]

Note here in the end how from the beginning of the chronicle that is called *Vox Clamantis*, together with the following chronicle, which is the *Tripertita*, covering the time of King Richard II up to his deposition, as well as the coronation of the most illustrious lord King Henry IV up the second year of his reign, according to the different turns of events I the author, though unworthy in comparison to other *pr5* authors, being long concerned especially over what was happening during this time in England, composed in a brief compendium a series of poems of essential reading concerning the various events that occurred. And now, weighed down in many ways as much by the burden of old age as of other ailments, I am not up to the task of writing distinctly about the chronicles any more and I intend to declare *pr10* my recusal, whose necessity is obvious, in what follows.

Henrici regis annus fuit ille secundus
    Scribere dum cesso, sum quia cecus ego.
Ultra posse nichil, quamuis michi velle ministrat,
    Amplius ut scribam non meus actus habet.
5   Scribere dum potui, studiosus plurima scripsi;
    Pars tenet hec mundum, pars tenet illa Deum:
Vana tamen mundi mundo scribenda reliqui,
    Scriboque finali carmine vado mori.
Scribat qui veniet post me discrecior alter,
10   Ammodo namque manus et mea penna silent.
Sic quia nil manibus potero conferre valoris,
    Est michi de precibus ferre laboris onus.
Deprecor ergo meis lacrimis, vivens ego cecus,
    Prospera quod statuas regna futura, Deus,
15   Daque michi sanctum lumen habere tuum. Amen.

[All Souls version]

Hic in fine notandum est qualiter, ab illa cronica que *Vox Clamantis* dicitur usque in finem istius cronice que *Tripertita* est, ego inter alios scribentes super hiis que medio tempore in Anglia contingebant, secundum varias rerum accidencias varia carmina, prout patet, que ad legendum necessaria sunt, notabiliter conscripsi. Sed nunc, quia ulterius scribere non sufficio, excusacionis mee causam scriptis   *pr5* subsequentibus plenius declarabo.

Quicquid homo scribat finem natura ministrat,
    Que velud umbra fugit, nec fugiendo redit;
Illa michi finem posuit, quo scribere quicquam
    Ulterius nequio, sum quia cecus ego.
5   Posse meum transit, quamuis michi velle remansit;
    Amplius ut scribat hoc michi posse negat.
Carmina dum potui, studiosus plurima scripsi;
    Pars tenet hec mundum, pars tenet illa Deum.
Vana tamen mundi mundo scribenda reliqui,
10   Scriboque mentali carmine verba Dei.
Quamuis exterius scribendi deficit actus,
    Mens tamen interius scribit et ornat opus.

Sic quia de manibus nichil amodo scribo valoris,
    Scribam de precibus que nequit illa manus.
15   Hoc ego, vir cecus, presentibus oro diebus,
    Prospera quod statuas regna futura, Deus,
    Daque michi sanctum lumen habere tuum. Amen.

That was the second year of King Henry IV
    When I stopped writing, because I am blind.
My ability serves me no further, although my will does,
    But my physical agency lacks the means to write more.
5   While I was able to write, I wrote very many things with zeal;
    This part clings to the world, that part clings to God.
Nevertheless I have left to the world its vanities still to be written,
    And with a final poem I write and I go to die.
Let other, wiser men who come after me write on,
10   For from this time forth my hand and my pen will be silent.
Thus, because with my hands I can compose nothing of value,
    It is my task to bear the burden of my toil in my prayers.
Therefore I plead with my tears, living and blind,
    That you make our kingdoms prosperous in the future, O God,
15   And grant that I receive Your holy light. Amen.

[All Souls Version]

Here in the end it is to be noted how, from the chronicle that is called *Vox Clamantis* to the end of the chronicle that is called *Tripertita*, I notably composed different poems, which are necessary to read, in the midst of others writing about the things that happened in England in this intervening time, according to the different turns of events, as is obvious. But now, because I am not up to the task of writing any more, I will explain the reason for my recusal more fully in the following writings. *pr1–5*

To whatever a man writes, Nature applies a limit
    Which flees like a shadow, nor returns having fled;
She has placed a limit on me, so that I am unable
    To write any longer, because I am blind.
5   Although my will remains, my ability passes;
    It declines to write any more.
When I was able, I wrote many poems with zeal;
    One part deals with the world, the other with God.
But I have left to the world its vanities still to be written,
10   And in a poem of my imagination I write the words concerning God.
Although the act of writing externally now fails me,
    Still my mind writes within me and adorns the work.

Thus because I can write nothing further with my hands,
    I will write with my prayers what my hand cannot.
15   This is what I, a blind man, pray for in these present days,
    That You make our kingdoms prosperous in the future, O God,
    And grant that I receive your holy light.

11. PRESUL OUILE REGIS

(see note)

Presul, ovile regis ubi morbus adest macularum,
Lumina dumque tegis, tenebrescit pestis earum.
Mune pericla gregis, patuit quia stella minarum,
Unde viam regis turbat genus insidiarum.
5 Velle loco legis mundum nunc ducit avarum,
Sic ubicumque legis, nichil est nisi cordis amarum;
    Quod maneat clarum, stat modo dulce parum.

12. UNANIMES ESSE QUI SECULA

Unanimes esse qui secula duxit ad esse
Nos iubet expresse, quia debet amor superesse;
Lex cum iure datur, pax gaudet, plebs gratulatur,
Regnum firmatur, ubi verus amor dominatur.
5 Sicut yemps florem, divisio quassat amorem,
Nutrit et errorem quasi pestis, agitque dolorem.
Quod precessit heri docet ista pericla timeri,
Ut discant veri sapientes secla mederi.
Filius ipse Dei, manet in quo spes requiei,
10 Ex meritis fidei dirigat acta rei.
    Diligamus invicem.

13. CULTOR IN ECCLESIA

Cultor in ecclesia qui, deficiente sophia,
    Semina vana serit, messor inanis erit.
Hii set cultores sunt quorum semina mores
    Ad messem Cristi, plura lucrantur ibi.
5 Qui cupit ergo bonus celorum lucra colonus,
    Unde lucrum querat, semina sancta serat.
Qui pastor Cristi iusto cupit ordine sisti
Non sit cum Cristo Symon mediator in isto.
Querat pasturam pastor sine crimine puram,
10 Nam nimis est vile pascat si Symon ovile.
Per loca deserta, quo nulla patet via certa,
Symon oves ducit, quas Cristo raro reducit.

11. PRELATE

☞   **O** shepherd, a disease of spots affects the king's sheepfold,
        And while you hide the light their plague darkens all.
        Defend the flock from dangers, for the menacing star has appeared,
        By which an invidious race lays ambush on the king's highway.
5   Greed, not law, now leads an avaricious world;
        Thus, wherever you cast your gaze there is nothing but bitterness of heart;
            As should be clear, little sweetness remains.

12. TO BE OF ONE MIND HE WHO THE AGES

    To be of one mind He who the ages brought into being
    Orders us expressly, because Love should be supreme;
    Law and rights are observed, peace rejoices, the people are happy,
    The kingdom is strong, where true Love rules.
5   As winter destroys the flower, so division destroys love,
    And like the plague fosters error and brings on grief.
    What happened yesterday teaches that such dangers are to be feared,
    So that men of true wisdom can learn to heal the times.
    May the Son of God himself, in whom rests our hope of repose,
10   From the merits of faith give direction to deeds and events.
        Let us love each other.

13. THE HUSBANDMAN IN THE CHURCH

    The husbandman in the Church, who, when wisdom is lacking,
        Sows seeds of vanity, will be a harvester of nothing.
    But those husbandmen whose seeds are good morals
        Reap great gains there for Christ's harvest.
5   Therefore let the good farmer who desires profits of Heaven
        Sow seeds that are holy from which to await his gains.
    In one who desires to stand upright as Christ's shepherd
    Let not Simon be his mediator with Christ.
    Let the shepherd guiltlessly seek a pure pasture,
10   For the sheepfold where Simon feeds is excessively vile.
    Through the waste places, where no path lies open,
    Simon leads his sheep, which he seldom leads back to Christ.

14. DICUNT SCRIPTURE

Dicunt scripture memorare novissima vite;
Pauper ab hoc mundo transiet omnis homo.
Dat fortuna status varios, natura set omnes
Fine suo claudit, cunctaque morte rapit.
5   Post mortem pauci qui nunc reputantur amici
Sunt memores anime; sis memor ergo tue:
Da, dum tempus habes, tibi propria sit manus heres;
Auferet hoc nemo, quod dabis ipse Deo.

15. ORATE PRO ANIMA (ARMIGERI SCUTUM)

[Cotton, Harleian text (no poem)]

Orate pro anima Iohannis Gower. Quicumque enim pro anima ipsius Iohannis devote oraverit, tociens quociens mille quingentos dies indulgencie, ab ecclesia rite concessos misericorditer in Domino possidebit.

[Glasgow text and poem]

Orantibus pro anima Iohannis Gower, mille quingenti dies indulgencie misericor-diter in Domino conceduntur.

Armigeri scutum nichil ammodo fert sibi tutum,
Reddidit immo lutum, morti generale tributum.
Spiritus exutum se gaudeat esse solutum,
Est ubi virtutum regnum sine labe statutum.

14. THEY SAY IN SCRIPTURE

They say in Scripture to remember the end of life.
Everyone will pass from this world as a poor man.
Fortune gives various conditions, but Nature brings to an end
All with her own conclusion, seizing everything at death.
5   After your death few who are now considered friends
Will be mindful of your soul; therefore, you should be mindful of it yourself.
Give, while you have time, let your heir be your own hand;
No one will take away what you yourself give to God.

15. PRAY FOR THE SOUL

[Cotton, Harleian text (no poem)]

Pray for the soul of John Gower. For whoever devoutly prays for the soul of the said John will receive each time one thousand five hundred days of indulgence, mercifully granted in the Lord in due form by the Church.

[Glasgow text and poem]

To those praying for the soul of John Gower, one thousand five hundred days of indulgence are granted mercifully in the Lord.

The esquire's shield now no longer gives him protection,
For he has rendered up his clay, the common tribute of death.
May his spirit rejoice to be rid of it and freed,
Where the kingdom of virtues is established without stain.

TEXTUAL AND EXPLANATORY NOTES

ABBREVIATIONS: *CA*: Gower, *Confessio Amantis*; *CB*: Gower, *Cinkante Ballades*; *Cronica*: Gower, *Cronica Tripertita*; *CT*: Chaucer, *The Canterbury Tales*; *CVP*: Gower, *Carmen super multiplici viciorum pestilencia*; *IPP*: Gower, *In Praise of Peace*; **Mac**: Macaulay edition; *MO*: Gower, *Mirour de l'Omme*; *TC*: Chaucer, *Troilus and Criseyde*; **Thynne**: William Thynne, printer, *The Works of Geffray Chaucer* (1532) [prints *IPP* from Tr]; *Traitié*: Gower, *Traitié pour essampler les amantz marietz*; *VC*: Gower, *Vox Clamantis*.

All biblical citations are to the Vulgate text, and, unless otherwise noted, all biblical translations are from the Douai-Rheims. For manuscript abbreviations, see pp. 6–7.

1. DE LUCIS SCRUTINIO

Probably written ca. 1392–95 (see note to lines 79–80 below). The poem presents, albeit in truncated form, a critique of the Estates familiar from *MO* and *VC*; however, here the central metaphor of Light (i.e., the light of Christ's teaching, example, and divine grace) everywhere engulfed in darknesses of sin and ignorance (compare Aquinas, *Summa Theologica* II.i.Q.112.Art.5) intensifies the poet's anger at the state of the world. As Rigg (in Echard and Fanger, *Latin Verses*, p. xix) has noted, metaphor so sustained is uncommon in English Latin poetry, and here lends a poignancy to Gower's expressions of heartfelt sorrow not often encountered in earlier poems by other hands. Stockton (*Major Latin Works*, p. 36) has pointed out Gower's apparent agreement here with the Lollards on the need for kings to end the schism of the Church. (See note to line 4, below.) The form is Leonine hexameter (except the final line, a pentameter), rhyming disyllabically throughout, irregularly including unisonant couplets most frequent toward the end. Lines 102–03 are distichs (Carlson, "Rhyme").

The text presented here is based on S (lines 1–92) and C (lines 93–103). Other versions survive in E, H, and L.

Prose   "*Qui ambulat in tenebris nescit quo vadat.*" John 12:35. The quote provides the context for Gower's poem. On Palm Sunday Jesus speaks to the crowd in response to the question, "Who is this Son of Man?": "Jesus therefore said to them: Yet a little while, the light is among you. Walk whilst you have the light, that the darkness overtake you not. And he that walketh in darkness knoweth not whither he goeth. Whilst you have the light, believe in the light, that you may be the children of light" (John 12:35–36).

         suffocarunt. So Mac, emending from C, E, H, and L. S: *suoffocarunt.*

1 ff.   ☞ **Latin marginalia** in S: *Nota quod eorum lucerna minime clarescit quos in ecclesia per antipapam avaricia promotos ditescit.* ("Note that the light of them is least bright, who grow rich in the Church through the Anti-Pope promoting avarice.")

3   *Si Romam pergas.* By "Rome," Gower means the Church itself; like Englishmen
            generally, he did not recognize the Avignon papacy (see following note).

4   *Rome sunt duo pape.* The so-called Great Schism (1378–1453) began with the
            election of Urban VI in Rome and Clement VII in Avignon. Gower attacks
            Clement specifically in *VC* III.x.955–56, and in the Latin marginalia to *CA* Prol.
            194–99. Outrage at the schism, as the source of heresies such as Lollardy, is
            common in his work. (See *CA*, ed. Peck, vol.1, p. 294.)

6   *Sub modio . . . lucerna reiecta.* Compare Matthew 5:15: "neque accendunt
            lucernam, et point eam sub modio" ("neither do men light a candle and put it
            under a bushel, but upon a candlestick, that it may shine to all that are in the
            house"). Compare note to line 100, below.

            ☞ **Latin marginalia** in S: *Nota de luce prelatorum et curatorum* ("Note: On the light
            of prelates and curates").

8   *Simonis.* A Samaritan and erstwhile magician known for that reason as Simon
            "Magus," who as recorded in Acts 8:18–24 offered the disciples money for the
            power to command the presence of the Holy Ghost. From his offer and name was
            the sin of simony derived — commonly the buying and selling of Church benefits.
            Those wearing his *bulla* (technically a medallion or amulet, often of gold, worn
            by Roman boys during the Empire to indicate free status) would thus be in the
            service of Simon, i.e., simoniacs, whom Dante (*Inferno* 19) relegates to the eighth
            circle of Hell, as a type of Fraud. On the contemporary political resonances of
            wearing of a medallion indicative of allegiance, see note to lines 27–28, below.
            There is also a clear pun on papal "bulls" (edicts), so named because the leaden
            seals they bore assuring the document's papal authenticity resembled the *bullae*
            of Roman boys. Gower's imagination is frequently Dantesque: compare simon-
            iacs, here identified by papal seals/medallions around their necks, and *Inferno* 17,
            where usurers are told apart only by the "tasca" — money-bag bearing coat of
            arms of families, but also therefore of banking houses — each wears around his
            neck. Compare also *VC* III.xii.1005–64 and *CA* Prol. 204–41.

11   *de membris nil fore purum.* See note to line 19, below.

13 ff.   ☞ **Latin marginalia** in S: *De luce ordinis professi* ["On the light of those professing
            holy orders"]

13–38   Compare Gower's discussions of clerical orders in *MO*, lines 18421–21780, and
            VC III and IV.

19   *lucerne, iocus, ocia, scorta, taberne.* The "dark light" of present-day prelates
            encourages bodily pleasures — "joking, 'leisure,' feasting, and prostitutes";
            compare line 11, above, where the "caput obscurum" ["dark mind"] produces
            "nothing pure from the limbs" ["de membris nil fore purum"].

20–22   *velamen . . . turbida templum / Nebula perfudit.* For *velamen* ("veil"), see Exodus
            34:30–33, where Moses after receiving the Commandments from God on Sinai
            dons a "velamen" to prevent the reflected glory of his face from driving away the
            people, who at first flee his brightness; and 2 Corinthians13–16, where Paul

interprets Moses' action as preventing the people from receiving a true (i.e., unmediated) vision of the Lord: "sed usque in hodiernum diem, cum legitur Moyses, velamen positum est super cor eorum. Cum autem conversus fuerit ad Dominum, auferetur velamen" ("But even until this day, when Moses is read, the veil is upon their heart. But when they shall be converted to the Lord, the veil shall be taken away"); and, further, Matthew 27:51, Mark 15:38, and Luke 23:45, who describe the veil of the Temple torn asunder the moment Christ dies. Luke, who makes a point of the rending as attended by darkness, is especially relevant: "Et obscuratus est sol et velum temple scissum est medium" ("And the sun was darkened, and the veil of the Temple was rent in the midst"). For the "stormy cloud" engulfing the Temple, see 3 Kings (1 Kings) 8:10–13, describing the descent of the Lord into the newly finished Temple of Solomon: "et non poterant sacerdotes stare et ministrare propter nebulam: impleverat enim gloria Domini domum Domini" ("And the priests could not stand to minister because of the cloud: for the glory of the Lord had filled the house of the Lord"). Gower's complex metaphor depends upon a reversal of these passages, the last particularly (i.e., the only cloud in the Temple nowadays is not glorious but dark — it is true darkness, not an excess of light, which prevents today's priests from ministering); the key is line 21, *Sic perit exemplum lucis*, where the "model of light" is Christ, at whose execution by the unenlightened the veil of the temple was torn, and darkness descended — although paradoxically (like "Good" Friday) it is a darkness which should lead to conversion, and the taking-away (or rending) of the "veil upon their heart." See following notes to lines 23 and 24.

23   *Sic vice pastorum quos Cristus*. The metaphor of lines 20–22 is continued through an allusion to Vulgate Psalm 79:2: "Qui pascis Israel, ausculta, Qui ducis velem gregem Ioseph" ("Give ear, O shepherd of Israel, who leads Joseph like a sheep" — trans. mine); and 79:4: "Deus, restitue nos, Et serenum praebe vultum tuum, ut salvi simus" ("Convert [i.e., "restore"] us, O God, and shew us thy face: and we shall be saved"), where the echoes of Exodus 34:30–33 and 2 Corinthians 16 are intentional.

24   *chorum statuit iam mundus*. For the new "chorus of the world" compare Vulgate Psalm 137:4–5: "Confiteantur tibi, Domine, omnes reges terrae, Quia audierunt omnia verba oris tui; Et cantent in viis Domini, Quoniam magna est gloria Domini" ("May all the kings of the earth give glory to thee: for they have heard all the words of thy mouth. And let them sing in the ways of the Lord: for great is the glory of the Lord"). The allusion develops out of the associative commonality in the psalms of shepherds (see note to line 23) and music; here present conditions are in stark contrast to the chorus, invoked by the psalmist, of kings whose singing glorifies God. The reference provides a transition to the following passage, where attention is turned to secular rulers and the Church in relation to them.

25 ff.   ☞ **Latin marginalia** in S: *Nota quod, si regum lucerna in manu caritatis devocius gestaretur, ecclesia nunc divisa eorum auxilio discrecius reformaretur, eciam et incursus paganorum a Cristi finibus eorum probitate eminus expelleretur.* ["Note that if the light of kings was borne in the hand of the most devoted charity, their church that

now stands divided would restore more distinguished help, yet the assault of those pagans upon the countries of Christ expels honesty at a distance."]

26   *de guerra.* Possibly an allusion to the Hundred Years' War, but probably a generic response to the violence of the times.

27–28   *Ne periant . . . mater.* The schism divided kingdoms as well as prelates, e.g., France and most of the Spanish states supporting Clement VII, Portugal, the Holy Roman Empire, and England upholding Urban VI. ("Rome" here is generic for the Roman church.) Royal support would ensure authority for the "laws" (*leges*) of whichever pope a kingdom recognized. Line 28 is difficult; *pater* likely alludes to the pope, *mater* to the church (compare *IPP*, lines 239–41). The line could be understood "So that [each] pope might know which church [i.e., Rome or Avignon] believes his claim," with the "might makes right" implication from line 27 that the strength of partisan earthly kings, rather than God's will, decides papal "credibility" in a world so fallen.

29–30   *Scisma . . . viderent.* Suggests the "Two Swords," i.e., authority over men properly divided between the Holy Roman Emperor and the papacy: ideally, one should balance the other, but with the emperor now "asleep" (see *MO*, lines 22201–12), kings must act in unison to make matters right (compare *IPP*, lines 379–83).

33   *Teste paganorum bello.* Not a war of pagan deity against pagan deity, but of pagan believers against Christ: compare *IPP*, lines 190–96.

38   *Lumina namque David . . . titulavit.* Depending on the intention of *titulavit*: if understood as "appointed," perhaps a reference to 2 Kings (2 Samuel) 15, on David's confidence in, and betrayal by, Absolom and Achitiphel; if taken as "invoked," more probably Psalm 2. If the former, since the referent is "regentis" (line 36), probably an allusion to Richard's "evil counselors"; compare *VC* VII.vii. 567–636, with variants (although these lines were written much earlier); if the latter, the reference cloaks an admonition to Richard.

39 ff.   ☞ **Latin marginalia** in S: *De luce procerum.* ["On the light of the nobles."]

39–48   Compare *MO*, lines 23209–592, on the estate of the nobility.

42   *Nemo . . . de turbine grando.* Resonant of Osee 8:7: "Quia ventum seminabunt, Et turbinem metent" ("For they shall sow wind and reap a whirlwind"); "they" refers to "princes" ["principes"] in 8:4: "Ipsi renaverunt, et non ex me; Principes exstiterunt, et non cognovi; Argentum suum et aurum suum fecerunt sibi idola, Ut interirent" ("They have reigned, but not by me: they have been princes, and I knew not: *of their silver and their gold they have made idols to themselves, that they might perish*" — italics mine).

49 ff.   ☞ **Latin marginalia** in S: *De luce militum et aliorum qui bella sequntur.* ["On the light of the knights and others who wage war."]

49–54   Compare *VC* V.viii and *MO*, lines 23593–24180, on the estate of knights and men-at-arms.

55 ff.   ☞ **Latin marginalia** in S: *De luce legistarum.* ["On the light of the law."]

55–62   Compare *MO*, lines 24181–25176, and *VC* VI.i–v, on the estate of men of law.

57   *Mammona*. Aramaic: "riches," worldly goods. See Matthew 6:24; Luke 16:13 and 16:9.

63 ff.   ☞ **Latin marginalia** in S: *De luce mercatorum*. ["On the light of the merchants."]

63–72   Compare *MO*, lines 25177–26604, on the estate of merchants.

65–66   *Contegit usure . . . similatum*. The portrait of "usure" is traditional of avarice (see, e.g., *Piers Plowman* B.5.187–97); hence, "quem diues habet similatum" can be read: "the avaricious are all alike under the skin." See *VC* V.xii.703–834 and *MO*, lines 7213–7344 on Usury, the third daughter of Avarice.

67   *Si dolus . . . sigilla*. That is, "if documents could be falsified successfully."

73 ff.   ☞ **Latin marginalia** in S: *De luce vulgari, que patriam conseruat*. ["On the light of the people, which should save the country."]

74–78   *Nam via vulgaris . . . turbidiores*. Compare Vulgate Psalm 118, which celebrates (or proclaims: "Praeconium legis divinae") the divine law, especially 118:105: "Lucerna pedibus meis verbum tuum, Et lumen semitis meis" ("Thy word is a lamp to my feet, and a light to my paths") and 118:1–5: "Beati immaculati in via, Quia ambulant in lege Domini. Beati qui scrutantur testimonia eius, In toto corde exquirunt eum. Non enim qui operantur iniquitatem In viis eius ambulaverunt. Tu mandasti mandata tua Custodiri nimis. Utinam dirigantur viae meae Ad custodiendas iustificationes tuas!" ("Blessed are the undefiled in the way [path]: who walk in the law of the Lord. Blessed are they that search his testimonies: that seek him with their whole heart. For they that work iniquity have not walked in his ways [paths]. Thou hast commanded thy commandments to be kept most diligently. O that my ways [paths] may be directed to keep thy justifications!" — my additions). The emphasis here is on lawlessness by the unreasoning commons; compare *VC* I.ix–x.

79–80   *Sunt et conducti . . . rescisa*. Depending on the exactitude of *assisa* (line 80), whether figurative, for courts generally, or specifically limited to assizes. If the latter, it perhaps alludes to Richard II; but more likely the former: compare Vulgate Psalm 118:85–86; and similar complaints against nobility who take kickbacks from "communs baratours" (*MO*, lines 23317–28); "hedgerow knights" ("chivaler de haie") who rig court sessions (*MO*, lines 23725–36); manipulated judges (*MO*, lines 24625–816); jurors (*MO*, lines 25009–128); and "Covoitise" in the courtroom (*MO*, lines 6205–28). *Assisa* also completes Leonine rhyme with *rescisa* (line 80). See also note to *CVP*, lines 246–65, below.

88   *orbis iter sine luce*. Compare Vulgate Psalm 118:29 ("viam iniquitatis," "the path of iniquity") and note to line 96, below.

89 ff.   ☞ **Latin marginalia** in S: *Hic in fine tenebras deplangens pro luce optinenda Deum exorat*. ["Here in the end, mourning the darkness, he pleads for the light of God to prevail."]

92   *Cecos . . . tango.* Compare Vulgate Psalm 118:82: "Defecerunt oculi mei in elo-
        quium tuum" ("My eyes have failed for thy word") and 118:123: "Oculi mei
        defecerunt in salutare tuum" ("My eyes have fainted [failed] after your salvation"
        — my addition). Assuming composition ca. 1392, Macaulay rightly notes that
        Gower must be speaking figuratively; though he might have begun losing his
        eyesight "we must not assume that the author is referring to any physical blind-
        ness" (4.418).

93–103 The text of S ends at line 92, where a leaf is missing. The remainder of the text
        given here is from C.

96   *Nunc iter attendo.* Compare Vulgate Psalm 118:30 ("viam veritatis," "the path of
        truth") and the repetition of *iter* here from lines 88 and 94.

97   *Tu . . . creasti.* Compare Genesis 1–5.

98   *Crimina . . . dones.* Compare Vulgate Psalm 118:130: "Declaratio sermonem
        tuorum illuminat" ("The declaration of thy words giveth light") and 118:132–33:
        "Aspice in me, et miserere mei, Secundum iudicium diligentium nomen tuum,
        Gressus meos dirige secundum eloquium tuum, Et non dominetur mei omnis
        iniustitia" ("Look upon me and have mercy on me: according to the judgment
        of them that love thy name. Direct my steps according to thy word: and let no
        iniquity have dominion over me").

100   *Confer candelam.* Compare note to line 6, above; i.e., Christ as "candle" of faith:
        compare line 103.

102   *adhibit.* So C, H. Mac reads *adibit.*

2. CARMEN SUPER MULTIPLICI VICIORUM PESTILENCIA

Written probably mid-1396, although possibly as late as mid-1397 (see note to Prose 6,
below), *Carmen super multiplici viciorum pestilencia* is, after *VC* and *Cronica,* Gower's longest
Latin poem. It has close connections with *VC* VII.ix–xvi, sharing a central metaphor of phys-
ical decay and disease as emblematic of spiritual corruption, either of the individual (*VC*)
or, as here, of the Church and State. The poem particularly utilizes "plague" as a stand-in
for Lollardy. Fisher (*John Gower,* p. 128) associates it with "the outbreak of Lollard activity"
of 1395, and may be correct, at least about Gower's inspiration: in January of that year,
during parliament session, twelve-point manifestoes were posted on the doors of West-
minster Hall and St. Paul's by Lollards; a journey to the king in Ireland by Archbishop
Arundel and the bishop of London in February may have been to discuss the situation. In
any case, the king came home (compare Walsingham, *Chronica Monasterii S. Albani,* p. 173,
and *Historia Anglicana* 2.216–17). Parliament took matters seriously enough to grant the
king a tenth (i.e., a tenth part of the taxes raised that year) on 17 February for use against
the Lollards (*Chronica Monasterii S. Albani,* p. 173, and *Rotuli Parliamentorum* 3.329). The
1381 Rising provoked a near-immediate response from Gower — the so-called *Visio* as a new
first book for *VC*; conditions, and a similar responsiveness, seem analogous here. The sug-
gestion (by Coffman, "John Gower, Mentor," p. 955) that the poem is unfinished because
only three of the cardinal sins (Pride, Lust, and Avarice) are mentioned seems a logical con-
clusion, but in the end must be dismissed as conjecture, in the absence of evidence (Fisher,

John Gower, p. 128). The structure has been called "experimental" (Carlson, "Rhyme") for its mixing of disyllabic couplet-rhyme Leonine hexameters characteristic of *Cronica* and unrhymed elegiac distichs, the latter in several instances borrowed verbatim from *VC* II.ix. Notable too is the "marking" of sections start and finish with disyllabic-rhyming Leonine hexameters ending with a similarly rhymed pentameter.

Carmen super multiplici viciorum pestilencia has the widest distribution of the minor poems, being attached as follows to manuscripts of *CA*: T_2, B, Λ, P_2, F, H_2, K; and of *VC*: S, G, C, H, E_1, L, L_2. The text presented here is based on S.

8	*continuatur*. So Mac, emending from C, E, H, L, F, and B. S: *continiatur*.
11	*variatur*. Septicemia causes the skin of plague victims to become covered with bruises at the end stages of the disease. Compare *O Deus immense*, line 31, below.
Prose 1	*Putruerunt . . . insipiencie*. Macaulay (4.417) compares the passage to Vulgate Psalm 37:6: "Putruerunt et corruptae sunt cicatrices meae, A facie insipientiae meae" ("My sores are putrefied and corrupted, because of my foolishness").
Prose 4	*procurator*. S: *at* added above the line.
Prose 6–7	*Anno . . . vicesimo*. The twentieth year of Richard II's reign spanned 22 June 1396 to 21 June 1397. The date is also given in line 313, below.
Prose 8	*demonis*. See note to line 20, below.
13	*ad*. So Mac, emending from C, E, H, L, F, and B. S omits.
15	*plebs . . . resignat*. I.e., the Rising of 1381. Fisher remarks (*John Gower*, p. 129) that "order, not theology, is the real concern of the poet" here. See following note.
16	*laicus*. I.e., the Lollards. Although "Lollards" were from every social class, the dual assumptions, as here, of their being both commoners and rebels were widely held. See *Chronicon Angliae*, pp. 310–11, 320–21. The accusations were enhanced by the revolt of 1381, which Walsingham attributed to Archbishop Sudbury's failure to suppress Wyclif and his followers adequately, even claiming that John Ball himself was a Wycliffite. As Aston notes, "opinions once lodged are themselves historical facts: and, as such, may influence events" (*Lollards and Reformers*, p. 7).
20–23	*Lollia . . . fidem*. Compare Matthew 13:24–25 (and following): "Aliam parabolam proposuit illis, dicens: Simile factum est regnum caelorum homini, qui seminavit bonum semen in agro suo: cum autem dormirent homines, venit inimicus eius, et superseminavit zizania in medio tritici, et abiit" ("Another parable he proposed to them saying: The kingdom of heaven is likened to a man that sowed good seed in his field. But while the men were asleep, his enemy came and oversowed cockle among the wheat and went his way"). "Zizania" was understood as "lolium"; compare Isidore, *Etymologiae* XVII.9.106: "Zizania, quam poetae . . . lolium dicunt" ("Zizania, which the poets call . . . *lolium*" — my trans.); and *VC* IV.xxii.1083: "Sub triciti specie zizannia sepe refundunt" ("They frequently repay one with tares [cockle] under the guise of wheat" — trans. Stockton). Christ

explains the parable, Matthew13:37–39: "Qui seminat bonum semen, est Filius hominis. Ager autem est mundus. Bonum vero semen, hi sunt filii regni. Zizania autem, filii sunt nequam. Inimicus autem, qui seminavit ea, est diabolus" ("He that soweth the good seed is the Son of Man. And the field is the world. And the good seed are the children of the kingdom. And the cockle are the children of the wicked one. *And the enemy that sowed them is the devil*" — my italics). Compare prose heading, "demonis," above, line 29, below, and following note.

24   *apostata primus.* By "apostates" Gower means those who (Luke 8:13) "ad tempus credunt, et in tempore tentationis recendunt" ("believe for a while and in time of temptation they fall away"); hence, the devil, here conceived as Lucifer, the "first apostate": compare *CA* 8.10–12: "Bot Lucifer he putte aweie, / With al the route apostazied / Of hem that ben to him allied"; and *VC* IV.xxii.1019–20: "Est deus, est mundus, est demon apostate, cuius / Ordine transgressus fert sibi frater onus" ("There is God, there is the world, and there is the Devil Apostate, / In whose ranks the friar bears the burden of sin" — trans. Stockton). Here Lollards receive accusations aimed at friars in *VC*: see note to lines 36–37, below.

29   *lollia.* See note to lines 20–23, above.

30   *novam sectam.* The Lollards.

32   *Ioviniani.* Jovinian (d. ca. 405), condemned for heresy in 390, was bitterly attacked by Jerome in *Adversus Jovinianum* (ca. 393), which now, ironically enough, is the best source of Jovinian's ideas, which apparently opposed such basic tenets of Christian doctrine as the superiority of virginity, the hierarchy of sins, and the meritorious inequalities of punishment and heavenly reward; Jovinian also did not maintain the perpetual virginity of the Virgin Mary. But it is unlikely that any of these ideas specifically are meant here, or that Gower intends a one-to-one correspondence to Wyclif (whom Gower never names in any known work). More probable is Jovinian's service here and elsewhere in Gower's writing as a prototypical schismatic who gained a following (for which he was condemned), in that way resembling Lucifer and Lollards, sowers of bad seed: another such heretic for Gower is Arius. Compare *VC* VI.xix.1267: "Nunc nouus est Arius, nouus est quasi Iouinianus; / Dum plantant heresim, dant dubitare fidem" ("Now there is a new Arius, now there is a new Jovinian, so to speak; / since they both sow heresy, they cause faith to doubt" — trans. Stockton).

35   *palleat.* So S, C, H, L, and B. Mac emends to *palliet* based on F.

36–37   *Sub grossa lana . . . tegit.* Verbatim from *VC* IV.xxii.1047–48, where the lines describe the fraudulence of friars. The passage is identified by Beichner ("Gower's Use of the *Aurora*," p. 592) as verbatim from Peter of Riga's *Aurora* (his *Biblia versificata*), Deut. 89–90. "Coarse wool" probably refers to the Lollards' simple clothing, as in *VC* it did to friars' habits; hiding "fine linen" underneath, however appropriate a critique for friars, strikes some (e.g., Stockton, *Major Latin Works*, p. 34) as "far-fetched" and — given their abhorrence of worldly wealth — hardly Lollard practice. Gower was borrowing a metaphor here, not a snapshot; see note to line 24, above.

38   *Fermento veteri . . . acervum.* Compare Matthew 16: 11–12: "Quare non intelligitis, quia non de pane dixi vobis: Cavete a fermento pharisaeorum et sadducaeorum? Tunc intellexerunt quia non dixerit cavendum a fermento panum, sed a doctrina pharisaeorum et sadducaeorum" ("Why do you not understand that it was not concerning bread I said to you: Beware of the leaven of the Pharisees and Sadducees? Then they understood that he said not that they should beware of the leaven of bread, but of the doctrine of the Pharisees and Sadducees"); and 1 Corinthians 5:6–8: "Nescitis quia modicum fermentum totam massam corrumpit? Expurgate vetus fermentum, ut sitis nova conspersio, sicut estis azymi. Etenim Pascha nostrum immolatus est Christus. Itaque epulemur: non in fermento veteri, neque in fermento malitiae et nequitiae: sed in azymis sinceritatis et veritatis" ("Know you not that a little leaven corrupteth the whole lump? Purge out the old leaven, that you may be a new paste, as you are unleavened. For Christ our pasch is sacrificed. Therefore, let us fast not with the old leaven, nor with the leaven of malice and wickedness: but with the unleavened bread of sincerity and truth").

40   *Dum magis incantat . . . aures.* Gower has in mind the serpent "Aspidis" which covers its ears to escape "enchantement" by its hunter (*CA* 1.463–80); the "Sirenes," against whose singing Ulysses stopped the ears of his mariners lest they take for "Paradys, / Which after is to hem an helle" (*CA* 1.502–03); or both, since in *CA* one tale directly precedes the other, and *incantat* implies enchantment through (hypnotic) song.

52–53   *Argumenta fides . . . capi.* Compare Luke 1:52: "Deposuit potentes de sede, / Et exaltavit humiles" ("He hath put down the mighty from their seat, / And exalted the humble"); and Aquinas, *Summa Theologica* II.ii.Q.1.Art.4.

56–57   *Ut solus . . . opus.* Verbatim from *VC* II.ix.439–40; the larger subject of the chapter from which these and the following excerpts were taken is "quilibet debet firmiter credere, nec ultra quam decet argumenta fidei investigare" ("everyone ought firmly to believe, and not investigate the grounds of faith more than is proper" — trans. Stockton). The immediate subject of lines 439–40 is the Creation; see notes to lines 60–75, 76–77, below.

60–75   *Leticiam luctus . . . fidem.* Verbatim from *VC* II.ix.445–60.

64   *sacri flatus.* Compare "spiritus vitae" Genesis 2:7, 6:17, 7:15.

66   *Cum . . . nosse.* Compare Mark 13:33: "Videte, vigilate, et orate: nescitis enim quando tempus sit" ("Take heed, watch and pray. For ye know not when the time is").

76–77   *Committat fidei . . . fides.* Verbatim from *VC* II.ix.465–66.

84–85   *Sic incarnatum . . . homo.* For Gower, this is the crowning example of miracle accessible only through faith; there is no suggestion, however, that Gower thought Lollards denied the Virgin Birth.

85–86   *Virginis . . . revereri.* Identified by Beichner ("Gower's Use of the *Aurora*," p. 593) as verbatim from *Aurora*, Exod. 85–86.

86   *Pete, crede, stude, revereri.* Compare Vulgate Psalm 36:3–5 and note to line 87, below.

87   *lex*: Compare line 86, above, and Matthew 22:37: "Diliges Dominum Deum tuum ex toto corde tuo, et in tota anima tua, et in tota mente tua" ("Thou shalt love the Lord thy God with thy whole heart and with thy whole soul and with thy whole mind").

90   *Tempore Ricardi.* Compare Coffman, "John Gower, Mentor," p. 958: "Gower, after expressing grave concern over the decay of orthodoxy in religion through Lollardy, exhorts Richard to accept the authority and assume the responsibility to suppress this heresy."

96   *Radix peccati . . . scelerati.* Compare *CA* 1.580–81: "The ferste of hem thou schalt believe / Is Pride, which is principal"; *MO*, line 1045: "Orguil, des autres capi-teine" ("Pride, the leader of the others" — trans Wilson); and Aquinas, *Summa Theologica* II.i.Q.84,Art.2.

97   *Ex quo dampnati.* Compare Apocalypse 12:9: "et proiectus est in terram, et angeli eius cum illo missi sunt" ("And [Satan] was cast unto the earth: and his angels were thrown down with him").

98–99   *Michaelis / Ensis.* Compare Apocalypse 12:7: "Michael et angeli eius praelia-bantur cum dracone" ("Michael and his angels fought with the dragon"); and *MO*, lines 3733–45. For the sword, compare Genesis 3:24.

108–09 *Laus ibi non . . . eorum.* Richard's court was criticized for following continental fashions: compare *Richard the Redeless* 3.110–225. That pride led kings and courts to extravagant dress was, however, a commonplace: compare Hoccleve's criticism of court fashion under Henry IV, *Regiment of Princes*, lines 414–511.

120–21 "*Elatas mentes . . . amavit.*" No psalm of David contains precisely this statement; however, compare Vulgate Psalm 34, in which David writes against the injustice of those who persecute him.

124–25 *Acherontis, / Unde bibunt vani mortem.* No tradition links Acheron with either a deadly fountain or, specifically, with the vain; compare Virgil's *Aeneid* 6.295–330 and Dante's *Inferno* 3.71–81, 124. As the boundary river of hell it may figure here to indicate hell in general; also, "fontis / Acheronitis" completes a couplet and so may have been linked for rhyming purposes: compare *CA* 5.1109–12: "Be Lethen and be *Flegeton*, / Be Cochitum and *Acheron*, / The whiche, after the bokes telle, / Ben the chief flodes of helle."

126   *stat.* So Mac, adding from C, E, H, L, F, and B. S omits.

138–39 *Sunt que maiores humilis . . . minores.* On Humility as the virtue balancing Pride, compare *MO*, lines 10177–12614; *CA* 1.3284 ("Humilite most worth of alle") and 1.3296–97 ("What lest is worth of alle thinges, / And costeth most . . . is Pride").

147   *nec ibi sua debita soluit.* Compare 1 Corinthians 7:2–4: "propter fornicationem autem unusquisque suam uxorem habeat, et unaquaeque suum virum habeat. Uxori vir debitum reddat: similiter autem et uxor viro. Mulier sui corporis po-

testatem non habet, sed vir. Similiter autem et vir sui corporis potestatem non habet, sed mulier" ("But for fear of fornication, let every man have his own wife: and let every woman have her own husband. Let the husband render the debt to his wife: and the wife also in like manner to the husband. The wife hath not power of her body: but the husband. And in like manner the husband also hath not power of his own body: but the wife"). The idea of a sexual "debt" owed each other by husbands and wives was a common notion: see, for example, the opinion of Chaucer's Wife of Bath (*CT* III[D]152–61), or his Parson's lecture on the three fruits of marriage — procreation, satisfaction of nature, and avoiding fornication (*CT* X[I]939–42).

151   *Philosophus quidam.* It is unlikely any specific "philosopher" is intended here; compare *Traitié* VI–XVI, where the succession of ballades recounts a similar list of bad ends resulting from adultery.

175–76   *Libera set racio . . . Deo.* Reason and Conscience act together in *MO*, lines 10032–176, inducing God to marry his seven daughters, the Virtues, to Reason, to engender more virtues and combat the seven Vices and their offspring.

180–81   *Appetit in carne . . . fugiendus.* Verbatim from *VC* VI.xii.861–62.

182   *facta David.* I.e., his adultery with Bethsabee; compare 2 Kings (2 Samuel) 11–12.

183   *Consilio Balaam.* Compare Numbers 31:16: "Nonne istae sunt, quae deceperunt filios Israel ad suggestionem Balaam, et praevaricari vos fecerunt in Domino super peccato Phogor, unde et percussus est populus?" ("Are these not they, that deceived the children of Israel, by the counsel of Balaam, and made you transgress against the Lord by the sin of Phogor for which also the people was punished?"). The "sin of Phogor" was fornication: compare Numbers 25:1, 25:8, 25:14–15, 25:18.

193   *fictilis etas.* Compare *VC* VII.iii.135–74, where the sin of the age is said to be sexual excess (e.g., "Sic sacra scripta caro conscribitur undique mundo" ["The world everywhere inscribes carnal lust as holy writ" — trans. Stockton]). The larger image is the statue of Nebuchadnezzar's dream: compare *CA* Prol. 585–662; Daniel 2:31–45.

197–98   *Cecus amor . . . amans.* Compare *Ecce patet tensus.* Blind Cupid, with the power to blind his disciples, is common in Gower. E.g., *CA* Prol.47, 4.1732, 8.2268, and, especially, 8.2788–2808, where the blind god "which may noght se" gropes the wound of the stupified Amans to remove the fiery dart, whereupon the protagonist regains his vision and "John Gower" identity.

199   *Pendula . . . dolore.* Compare Ovid, *Metamorphoses* 7.826: "Credula res amor est: subito conlapsa dolore" ("Love is a credulous thing: struck suddenly with pain," used verbatim *VC* V.iii.165).

203–04   *Cum viciis . . . homo.* Compare 1 Corinthians 6:18: "Fugite fornicationem" ("Fly fornication").

210   *mortis.* So Mac, emending from C, E, H, L, F, and B. S: *cordis.*

211–14   *Oscula fetor . . . madet.* Compare *VC* VII.x.765–78; here, however, and throughout *VC* VII, Gower's concern is with bodily corruption post mortem.

213–14   *Occupat . . . madet.* Compare Proverbs 14:13: "Risus dolore miscebitur, / Et extrema gaudii luctus occupant" ("Laughter shall be mingled with sorrow, / And mourning taketh hold of the end of joy").

215   *voluptas.* So Mac, emending (unnoted), from C, E, H, L, F, and B. S: *vluptas.*

217   *statutum.* S: *tu* added above the line by a later hand.

218–19   *Quo caro . . . vorabit.* Compare Genesis 3:19: "In sudore vultus tui vesceris pane, donec revertaris in terram de qua sumptus es: quia pulvis es et in pulverem reverteris" ("In the sweat of thy face shalt thou eat bread till thou return to the earth, out of which thou wast taken: for dust thou art, and into dust thou shalt return").

231   *Ex vicio . . . mali.* Compare 1 Timothy 6:10: "Radix enim omnium malorum est cupiditas" ("For the desire of money is the root of all evils"). Chaucer's Pardoner takes this as the text for his exhortation; see Chaucer's *CT* VI(C)333–34.

232–34   *Nemo Dei nomen . . . statuit.* Compare Exodus 20:7: "Non assumes nomen Domini Dei tui in vanum" ("Thou shalt not take the name of the Lord thy God in vain"); and 20:16: "Non loqueris contra proximum tuum falsum testimonium" ("Thou shalt not bear false witness against thy neighbor"). These are two of the Ten Commandments, the "Old Law" of Moses.

246–65   *Vendere iusticiam . . . fidem.* Compare *VC* VI.vi.445–62, especially 445: "Vendere iusticiam quid id est nisi vendere Cristum" ("What is it to sell justice but to sell Christ" — trans. Stockton). See also note to lines 79–80, above.

265   *Nunc modus . . . fidem.* This may be an oblique reference to Richard II's "*cartes blanches* involving admission of debt and guilt which he forced members of the opposition to sign" (Stockton, *Major Latin Works*, p. 40). See also *Cronica* III.67–72.

266   *Vox leuis . . . nuper.* Compare Genesis 27:22: "Accessit ille ad patrem, et palpato eo, dixit Isaac: Vox quidem, vox Iacob est: sed manus, manus sunt Esau" ("He came near to his father, and when he had felt him, Isaac said: The voice indeed is the voice of Jacob; but the hands are the hands of Esau"). By impersonating his brother, Jacob deprived Esau of his father's blessing; see note to lines 270–72, below.

270–72   *Ex dampno fratris . . . annos.* The allusion to the Jacob and Esau story continues here; see note to line 266, above.

276–77   *Quid modo . . . / Dicam?* Compare Matthew 6:3: "Te autem faciente eleemosynam, nesciat sinistra tua quid faciat dextera tua" ("And when thou dost alms, let not thy left hand know what thy right hand doth"). The play here is archly skilfull: because the right hand now takes bribes instead of giving alms, it has moved to (become) the left. The idea becomes proverbial. See Whiting, H61.

295   *Cum se nemo . . . sibi?* Not even a man's body belongs to him, for it too will decay after death. Compare *Orate pro anima*, below.

298   *Mammona*. Compare Matthew 6:24: "Non potestis Deo servire et mammonae"
           ("You cannot serve God and mammon"); and Luke 6:9–14.

302 ff.   ☞ **Latin marginalia** in S: *Salomon: Memorare novissima et inteternum non peccabis.*
           ("Solomon: Remember the newest [i.e., the last] things and you will not sin by
           the temporal.") The allusion is to the "Four Last Things": death, judgment,
           heaven, and hell. See *Dicunt scripture*, note to line 1.

305 ff.   ☞ **Latin marginalia** in S: *Idem: Omnia fac cum consilio et ineternum non penitebis.*
           ("Do all things with counsel and you will not repent the temporal.")

307   *Tempore presenti . . . genti*. By "the present time" Gower *may* have in mind pre-
           cisely the twentieth year of Richard II (June 1396 to June 1397), when he says
           he is writing *CVP* (line 312, below, and Prose, line 6, above), or he may be speak-
           ing more generally, as he does elsewhere: compare *VC* II.Pro.83–84: "Vox cla-
           mantis erit nomenque voluminis huius, / Quod sibi scripta novi verba doloris
           habet" ("And the name of this volume shall be *The Voice of One Crying*, because
           the work contains a message of the sorrow of today" — trans. Stockton). *VC* II
           was probably composed before 1381. See also note to line 314, below.

314   *Vox sonat in populo*. Compare Isaias 40:3: "Vox clamantis in deserto: / Parate
           viam Domini, / Rectas facite in solitudine semitas Dei nostri" ("The voice of one
           crying in the desert: Prepare ye the way of the Lord, make straight in the wil-
           derness the paths of our God"). See also note to line 307, above.

316   *Quem peperit . . . sacro*. Compare Luke 1:35: "Spiritus sanctus superveniet in te,
           et virtus Altissimi obumbrabit tibi" ("The Holy Ghost shall come upon thee,
           and the power of the Most High shall overshadow thee"). The tradition of the "Holy
           Breath" is not biblical, but developed from two sources: linguistic (*Spiritus /
           inspirare*, "to breathe" [compare the General Prologue of Chaucer's *Canterbury
           Tales*, I(A)5–6] and metaphoric (Christ as the Divine Logos, the Word of God,
           who in that way entered Mary through her ear at the angel's greeting).

3. EST AMOR

Est amor seems to have been written to celebrate Gower's marriage on 25 January 1398
to Agnes Groundolf, a fellow parishioner at St. Mary Overie and, as has been suggested by
Fisher (*John Gower*, p. 65) and others, also his nurse (Gower very likely being in his sixties,
although no birth record is known to exist). *Est amor* is commonly placed to conclude the
Traitié in the manuscripts, with minor variation in the headings; it also therefore appears in
most manuscripts containing *CA*: see Macaulay 1.lxxxv–lxxxvii and 1.392. The form is pre-
dominantly Leonine hexameter with disyllabic internal and end-rhyme, lines 1–15 in "-osa"
and lines 20–27 in "-orum." Lines 16–19, however, are elegiac distichs with internal rhymes
in "-guis" (lines 16–17) and couplet end-rhymes in "-or" and "-ita." In lines 18–19 the in-
ternal rhyme is also on "-ita." A form so mixed is not found in a closely related passage *VC*
(see below). Noting the change in form at line 19, and because a third (albeit less elaborate)
initial begins line 20, Macaulay (4.359) prints *Est amor* as two poems; Carlson ("Rhyme")
argues for a single poem in three distinct stanzas, as adopted here.

The text here is based on S and F.

1–15   Compare *VC* V.ii, where many of the same oxymora are used. In *VC*, however, the passage serves to condemn knights whose feats of arms are spurred by lust, "cuius passiones variis adinuicem motibus maxime contrariantur" ("the passions of which are highly at variance with each other, because of their mixed emotions" — trans. Stockton). The emotional turbulence of *Est amor*, ostensibly autobiographical and written in anticipation of his wedding, suggests feelings of groom for bride that would be surprising if Gower's relationship with Agnes was solely invalid and nurse. The source of the oxymora of *VC* and *Est amor* is quite likely Alan of Lille, *De Planctu Naturae*, met.V.

10   *tenebrosa.* So F, followed by Macaulay. S: *tenobrosa.*

16   *Magnus . . . clamor.* The metaphor is perhaps inspired by *De Planctu Naturae*, pros.V.

17   *ambiguis motibus.* Possibly suggests the planetary movement and influence of Venus; compare *CA* VIII.771–800, especially lines 777–80.

20–27   In S and F, copied as a separate stanza; in Tr, conjoined; see Macaulay 1.474.

20–21   *Lex docet auctorum . . . coniugiorum.* The authorities Gower may have had in mind might include 1 Corinthians 7:1–2: "Bonum est homini mulierem non tangere: propter fornicationem autem unusquisque suam uxorem habeat" ("It is good for a man not to touch a woman. But for fear of fornication, let every man have his own wife: and let every woman have her own husband"); or 1 Corinthians 7:9: "Quod si non se continent, nubant. Melius est enim nubere, quam uri" ("But if they do not contain themselves, let them marry. For it is better to marry than to be burnt"). The idea that, while virginity and chastity are more deserving, marriage is safest for most was a medieval commonplace: compare Whiting, W162, who traces versions to Alfred, ca. 900; and further Chaucer's Wife of Bath (*CT* III[D]52), Merchant (*CT* IV[E]1446–55), and Parson (*CT* X[I]915–17). See notes to lines 24–25 and lines 26–27, below.

24–25   *Hec est nuptorum . . . virorum.* The point is that marriage is of the flesh, an accommodation for mundane procreation necessitated only by the body. Compare Matthew 22:30: "In resurrectione enim neque unbent, neque nubentur: sed erunt sicut angeli Dei in caelo" ("For in the resurrection they shall neither marry nor be married, but shall be as angels of God in heaven"). See note to lines 20–21, above.

26   *Hinc vetus annorum Gower.* Fisher (*John Gower*, p. 46) and others following him suggest ca. 1330 as Gower's birth year, in which case he would have been about sixty-eight when he married Agnes Groundolf. This date is undocumented, however, and in fact Gower may have been much younger (see Yeager, "Gower in Winter").

26–27   *sub spe meritorum . . . thorum.* An interesting ambiguity is posed by conjoined idioms of faith and romance: Is the *spe meritorum* sought from wife or God? Does *tutus* continue to build upon the permissibility of sex in marriage or hint at impotence? Agnes' epitaph, doubtless written by Gower ("Quam bonitas, pietas, elemosina, casta voluntas" ["Whose goodness, piety, charity, willing chastity"]) and his assumed age might suggest the latter two options — but the choice of *sponsorum . . . thorum* sounds another, more virile note, particularly in context of lines 20–21. In *MO*, lines 17137–17748, Gower describes Matrimony as Chastity's third daughter and a guard against Adultery: clearly for him *casta* did not mean celibacy. See note to lines 20–21, above.

4. O DEUS IMMENSE

Usually ascribed to 1399, on the strength of the prose headings in S, C, H, and G (see Prose 1–2 note below) and the subject matter. However, while the headings themselves are clearly post-deposition (and in S, a manuscript given to Archbishop Arundel ca. 1402, apparently by Gower), dating is nonetheless difficult. Coffman ("John Gower, Mentor") argues the resemblance of Gower's advice to the thirty-three *gravamina*, or charges, leveled against Richard at the deposition "parliament" in September 1399 (see note to line 8, below). Yet similarity does not constitute evidence: Gower's advice is applicable to all kings, Henry IV included. The poem may have been composed, or at least begun, somewhat earlier, months before Henry's coup d'état, or even in 1398. Given Gower's habits of revision, particularly of work with political content, this uncertainty must always be allowed. (See notes to lines 99 and 103–04, below.) Indeed, Stockton (*Major Latin Works*, p. 36) may have it right, noting that when writing *O deus immense* Gower had "not yet given up hope for Richard." The prose headings of C, H, and G suggest as much also. The structure is predominantly Leonine hexameter with disyllabic rhyme and the occasional couplet, some of the latter infrequently with collateral rhyme (e.g., lines 5–6) as well; lines 95–104 are single-rhyme elegiac distich couplets. Line 104 is also pentameter.

The text here is based on S, read against C and H.

Prose 1–2   Two versions of the prose heading exist. S: *Carmen quod Iohannes Gower adhuc vivens super principum regimine ultimo composuit* ("A poem that John Gower, yet living, recently composed concerning the guidance of rulers"). C, H, G: *Carmen quod Iohannes Gower tempore regis Ricardi dum vixit ultimo composuit* ("A poem that John Gower recently composed in the time of King Richard, while he lived"). Macaulay, taking the S heading to be in Gower's hand, reads *dum vixit* and *adhuc vivens* as equivalents, to mean Gower wrote "with a view to future generations" (compare *Quia unusquisque*, line 4). Yet it is curious for a living poet to call attention to his own vitality. The fact that the positioning of *dum vixit* in C, H, and G clearly is applicable to Richard may provide clues to the meaning of S's *adhuc vivens*, the handwriting of the heading in S (not Gower's), and the date Gower began work on *O deus immense*.

2   *morosi*. Macaulay: "opposed here to '*viciosi*,'" citing *VC Epistle* line 57, trans. Stockton as "worthy." Here, however (and in line 57, below), it keeps its antique sense, complementary to *viciosi*.

5   *Quicquid delirant . . . Achivi*. Literally, *Achivi* = "Greeks" but the line, originally from Horace, *Epistles* I.ii.14, was proverbial in the fourteenth century, where *Achivi* was equated with the "comun people": compare *CA* VII.3930, beside which "Quicquid . . . Achivi" appears as a gloss. Compare also *MO*, lines 22825–48, and *VC* VI.vii.497 where, as Fisher has noted (*John Gower*, p. 131), the proverb has a different meaning. Gower's direct knowledge of Horace is doubt-

ful; rather, all of his few Horatian references (sometimes mistaken) indicate his reliance on a compendium.

7–8   A later hand has written *nota* ["note"] in the margin beside these lines in S.

7   *Laus et honor . . . legum.* Compare *MO*, lines 22234–36, 22240, and 22246–48.

8   *Ad quas iurati . . . vocati.* Presumably the coronation oath (compare *MO*, lines 22285–91) by which great contemporary store was set: in 1388 at the reconciliatory mass in Westminster Abbey, Richard repeated his oath and the Appellants theirs of homage. Charges that Richard violated his oath figured prominently in the *gravamina* presented against him in 1399, on which see Green, *Crisis of Truth*, pp. 234–35. Compare also Hoccleve's *Regiment of Princes*, lines 2192–98, advising the future Henry V.

10   *pax contulit oscula guerris.* Compare Vulgate Psalm 84:11: "Misericordia et veritas obviaverunt sibi; Iustitia et pax osculatae sunt" ("Mercy and truth have met each other: justice and peace have kissed"). Compare *MO*, lines 23082–88.

15–16   *Qui regit . . . recedit.* Compare *MO*, lines 22869–72.

19   *"Ve qui predaris."* Compare Isaias 33:1: Vae qui praedaris! Nonne et ipse praedaberis? Et qui spernis, nonne et ipse sperneris? Cum consummaveris depraedationem, depraedaberis; Cum fatigatus desieris contemnere, contemneris ("Woe to thee that spoilest! Shalt not thou thyself also be spoiled? And thou that despisest, shalt thou not thyself also be despised? When thou shalt have made an end of spoiling, thou shalt be spoiled: when being wearied thou shalt cease to despise, thou shalt be despised").

21–22   *Rex qui plus aurum . . . repente.* Compare *MO*, lines 22981–92.

28   *commune.* So Mac, emending from C and H. S: *comune.*

31–32   *pestis . . . crimine multo.* Compare *CVP*, line 11, above.

41   *vespere.* Vespers, or evensong, is the sixth canonical hour of the breviary. Gower warns against the king taking advice too quickly, which later may prove faulty.

49   *Cum laqueatur . . . altera.* Compare *Traitié* XV.7.

54   *Plebis et audire . . . redire.* Compare "vox populi, vox dei": *VC* III.Pro.11–13, III.xv.1267, VII.xxv.1470.

61   *Nomen regale . . . tibi.* Compare Marsilius of Padua (ca. 1324), *Defensor Pacis* I.18.3 for the same argument that royal authority proceeds from the people.

62   A later hand has written *nota* ("note") in the margin beside this line in S.

63–64   *Rex qui tutus . . . habebis.* Compare Job 36:10: "Revelabit quoque aurem eorum, ut corripiat; Et loquetur, ut revertantur ab iniquitate" ("He also shall open their ear to correct them: and shall speak, that they may return from iniquity").

68   *Saltem fortuna . . . una.* Compare Boethius, *De cons.* 2.pr.1. Fortune and her wheel are nearly ubiquitous in medieval literature and visual art: see Patch, *Goddess Fortuna*, and Kolve, *Chaucer and the Imagery of Narrative*, pp. 32, 327–28.

75–76	*Regia precedant . . . superno.* Compare Job 36:11–12. (See biblical text below.)

77   *Absque.* S: corrected from *Abque.*

77   *Absque Deo . . . cotidiana.* Compare *MO,* lines 23089–100.

79–80   *Rex sibi qui . . . carebit.* Compare Job 36:11–12: "Si audierint et observaverint, complebunt dies suos in bono, Et annos suos in Gloria: Si autem non audierint, Transibunt per gladium" ("If they [i.e., kings] shall hear, they shall accomplish their days in good, and their years in glory. But if they hear not, they shall pass by the sword").

83–85   A later hand has written *nota* ["note"] in the margin beside these lines in S.

85   *Quo caput . . . firmum.* Proverbial in the fourteenth century (compare Whiting, H254). Initially from Paul: compare Colossians 1:1, 1 Corinthians 12:12–28, and see further John of Salisbury, *Policraticus* V.3. Also compare *CA* 5.1038–40; *IPP,* line 260. On Gower's use of the figure generally, see Yeager, "Body Politic."

99   *pronus pro tempore . . . thronus.* Richard's throne might be said to have "declined" twice, in 1388 and 1399. It is difficult to imagine, if this is in fact a topical allusion, that the line was written in the earlier year; but sometime before Richard's assertion of power in 1397 is possible, however unlikely. On the other hand, it is equally difficult to imagine that the poem was composed entirely between August and September 1399, so the line probably should be seen as a late addition. See note to lines 103–04, below.

101   *Rex igitur . . . vadat.* Compare Vulgate Psalm 19:8: "Hi in curribus, et hi in equis: Nos autem in nomine Domini Dei nostri invocabimus" ("Some trust in chariots, and some in horses: but we will call upon the name of the Lord our God").

102   *ne rota versa cadat.* A neat conjunction of wheels: chariots' and Fortune's.

103–04 *Celorum regi . . . tegi.* That Richard ruled capriciously, without regard to statute, was a charge both in 1388 and 1399.

5. QUIA UNUSQUISQUE

Essentially a colophon summarizing Gower's three major poems, assumed to be Gower's own composition and written after 1399 since it mentions Richard's fall; but at that time Henry was not simply earl of Derby. (For the best reconciliation of its disparate history, see Nicholson, "Dedications.") There is some variation in placement and wording amongst the manuscripts, many being corrupt (e.g., a probable dropped line): see below, and Macaulay 3.550. Macaulay (4.418) pointed out that the description of *VC* seems "to include the *Cronica Tripertita* as a sequel." Pearsall ("Gower's Latin," pp. 24–25) noted the selective description of *CA* by way of warning against using *Quia* as an authorial summary. In five manuscripts containing the *Confesssio Amantis,* the colophon precedes *Eneidos bucolis* (see Appendix 1).

The text here is from S. Other versions survive in C, H, G, and F.

8   *Speculum Meditantis.* Macaulay 3.550: "'Speculum hominis' in all copies of the first recension. 'Speculum meditantis' over an erasure in the Glasgow MS of the *Vox Clamantis.*"

6. ECCE PATET TENSUS

Found only in Tr, where it follows *CB* and, despite an open-ended but nonetheless credible last line, has been taken by Macaulay and others following his lead to be incomplete. (A leaf is missing from the MS after line 36.) Rigg (*History of Anglo-Latin Literature*, p. 290) projects "a prayer for grace to avoid sin" as a likely finish, and suggests a date "before 1399." Carlson ("Rhyme") also considers it early work, based on the form — unrhymed elegiac distichs throughout, a number of its lines also turning up in *VC* (see below); but with nothing solid textually to indicate when Gower recombined them into a separate poem, nothing precludes his doing so in his late years, when demonstrably he was revising *VC*. Tr itself is datable ca. 1400; and pairing *Ecce patet* with *Est amor* as poems composed around 1398, the year of his marriage, achieves an interesting resonance. Many of the lines of this poem draw upon *VC* V.iii.147–92, a discussion of the wonder and danger of love; see the notes below.

3	*Omnia vincit amor*. Ultimately from Virgil, *Eclogues* 10.16; and compare *VC* V.iii.147, VI.xiv.999; and Chaucer, *CT* I(A)162.
10	*cunta*. So Tr. Mac reads *cuncta*.
15–17	*Sic amor . . . resoluit*. Verbatim *VC* V.iii.147–49.
21	*Sampsonis vires*. Judges 16:4–31.
	gladius . . . David. 2 Kings (2 Samuel) 11:2–12:24.
22	*laudis*. Clarified in the margin by a later hand.
	sensus . . . Salomonis. 3 Kings (1 Kings) 11:1–14.
23–24	*O natura . . . malum!* Verbatim *VC* V.iii.199–200.
25–26	*O natura . . . agi!* Verbatim *VC* V.iii.205–06.
27–28	*O natura . . . sequi!* Verbatim *VC* V.iii.201–02.

7. REX CELI DEUS

Of the three poems Fisher (*John Gower*, p. 99; and see further Carlson, "Gower's Early Latin") deemed the "laureate group" (along with *O recolende* and *H. aquile pullus*) probably the earliest, and likely Gower's tribute to Henry IV on or just after his "election," 30 September 1399. As Macaulay (4.416) observed, thirty-four of the fifty-six lines are "an adaptation of the original version" of *VC* VI.xviii, facilitating the swift composition required in the brief period between the deposition on 30 September and the coronation on 13 October. That the borrowed lines originally praised Richard II adds irony perhaps not lost on Henry and his supporters. The form is predominantly unrhymed elegiac distichs, although internal rhyme is present in lines 21–22 and unisonant internal and end-rhyme in "-a" appear in lines 36–37. More interesting are the final lines 51–56, clearly late: three unisonant couplets with internal and end-rhyme in "-i."

The text here is based on S, read against variants in C, H, G, H₃, and Tr.

Prose	*Sequitur carmen . . . glorificetur*. This heading generally precedes *Rex celi deus* in manuscripts including *Cronica*. In G and Tr, where *Cronica* is absent, *Rex celi deus*

follows *IPP*, and an alternative heading is used: *Explicit carmen de pacis commendacione, quod ad laudem et memoriam serenissimi principis domini Regis Henrici quarti suus humilis orator Iohannes Gower composuit. Et nunc sequitur epistola, in qua idem Iohannes pro statu et salute dicti domini sui apud altissimum devocius exorat.* ("Here ends the poem about the excellence of peace, which in praise and memory of the most serene prince of God, King Henry IV, his humble orator John Gower composed. And now follows an epistle, in which with the highest devotion the same John entreats for the health and well-being of his said lord.") On the connection between *IPP* and *Rex celi deus*, see note to line 39, below.

1–8   *Rex celi . . . ligavit ea.* Verbatim *VC* VI.xviii.1159*–66*. Compare Boethius, *De cons.* III.met.9, the most familiar statement of God as prime mover who, eternally stable himself, initiates motion elsewhere. Boethius' source is Aristotle; compare *Metaphysics* 12.6–10, *Physics* 8.6–10, and *On the Heavens* 3.2.

9   *Ipse caput regum.* That the godhead provides the model for the king as head of state is an idea frequently found in Gower's work; see Yeager, "Body Politic," and (on kingship generally) Peck, *Kingship*.

11   *Grata superveniens . . . nobis.* Compare the so-called Record and Process of the Renunciation of 30 September 1399, the official version of Henry's public "challenge" for the crown: "that god off his grace hath sent to me"; see *Chronicles of London*, p. 43. That Henry's accession resulted from divine grace was a cornerstone of Lancastrian propaganda. See lines 19, 21–25, and notes, below.

12   *O sine . . . fuit.* Compare Acts 15:16–17: "Post haec revertar, Et reaedificabo tabernaculum David, quod decidit: / Et diruta eius reaedicicabo, Et erigam illud: Ut requirant caeteri hominum Dominum, Et omnes gentes, super quas invocatum est nomen meum, Dicit Dominus faciens haec" ("After these things I will return and will rebuild the tabernacle of David, which is fallen down: and the ruins thereof I will rebuild. And I will set it up: That the residue of men may seek after the Lord, and all nations upon whom my name is invoked, saith the Lord, who doth these things"). See line 40, below.

12–15 *O sine . . . ab ymo.* As a description of the time prior to Henry's accession, when there was "no safety without disaster," these lines echo in all its hyperbole the Lancastrian version of the last two years of Richard's reign, 1397–99.

17–18 *Ex probitate . . . regit.* Compare Isaias 9:2: "Populus qui ambulabat in tenebris, Vidit lucem magnam; Habitantibus in regione umbrae mortis, Lux orta est eis" ("The people that have walked in darkness have seen a great light: to them that dwelt in the region of the shadow of death, light is risen"). Isaias 9 foretells the coming of Christ: compare 9:6: "Et factus est principatus super humerum eius" ("the government shall be upon his shoulder"), etc. See further lines 48–50, below.

25–26 *Qui tibi . . . frui.* Based on *VC* VI.xviii.1187*–88*: "Qui tibi prima dedit, confirmet Regna future, / Ut poteris magno magnus honore frui" ("May He Who gave you your first realms give you assurance of your future realms, in order that you as a great man can enjoy great honor" — trans. Stockton).

27–28   *Sit tibi progenies . . . solum*. In 1399 Henry IV had four living sons — Henry (eventually Prince of Wales and later Henry V), Thomas (eventually duke of Clarence), John (eventually duke of Bedford), Humphrey (eventually duke of Gloucester) — and two daughters, Blanche and Philippa. The sentiment is traditional for a poem of this type, but the abundance of Henry's grown children made it especially apt.

29   *Quicquid . . . alto*. Based on *VC* VI.xviii.1185*: "Que magis eterne sunt laudis summus ab alto."

31–32   *Omne quod . . . tuum*. Based on *VC* VI.xviii.1173*–74*: "Omne malum cedat, ne ledere posit, et omne / Est quod in orbe bonum, det deus esse tuum" ("May every evil vanish lest it have the power to do harm, and may God grant that every good which is on earth be yours" — trans. Stockton).

33   *Consilium nullum . . . iniqum*. Based on *VC* VI.xviii.1171*: "Consilium nullum te tangere posit iniquum" ("May no evil counsel have the power to influence you" — trans. Stockton). Bad advice from pernicious counselors was always a worry with regard to Richard II; here clearly it is a warning for Henry IV, in light of recent events.

35   *Absit avaricia*. Greed for his people's goods was central to several *gravamina* charged against Richard II at the deposition on 30 September 1399. On avarice elsewhere in Gower's work, see variously *MO*, lines 6181–7704; *CA* 5; *CVP*, lines 225–306.

36   *Nec queat . . . tua*. Based on *VC* VI.xviii.1172*: "Rex nec in hac terra proditor esse tua" ("O king, . . . may no betrayer of yours have the power to exist in this land" — trans. Stockton).

37–38   *Sic tua . . . tuas*. Verbatim from *VC* VI.xviii.1189*–90*.

39   *Nuper ut Augusti . . . Rome*. Based on *VC* VI.xviii.1179*: "Qualis et Augusti nuper preconia Rome" ("And may the shoutings of praise such as Augustus once had at Rome be yours anew" — trans. Stockton). *Augusti* is Augustus Caesar, whose accession ushered in the Pax Romana. Establishing peace as a goal of the new *imperium* underlies Gower's early addresses to Henry; compare lines 44, 47. See note to the *Prose* heading, above; and, further, *O recolende* and *IPP*, below.

40   *Anglia leta*. So S. Gower's Latin orthography allows a pun on *laeta* ("joyful") and *leta* (ruin). Both make sense in the context: see line 12, above.

40–41   *Concinat in gestis . . . nostro*. Verbatim from *VC* VI.xviii.1175*–76*.

45   *Augeat imperium . . . annos*. Based on *VC* VI.xviii.1181*: "Augeat imperium nostri ducis, augeat annos" ("Let the empire of our leader increase, let him increase his years" — trans. Stockton).

46   *Protegat . . . fores*. Verbatim from *VC* VI.xviii.1182*.

47   *Sit tibi pax . . . orbe*. Based on *VC* VI.xviii.1183*: "Stes magis, o pie Rex, domito sublimis in orbe" ("O good king, may you stand sublime in a vanquished world" — trans. Stockton).

48   *Cunctaque . . . tuis.* Verbatim from *VC* VI.xviii.1184*.

48–50   *Cunctaque sint humeris . . . queant.* See note to lines 17–18, above.

51   *Cordis amore . . . paravi.* Based on *VC* VI.xviii.1193*: "Hec tibi que, pie Rex,
          humili de corde paraui" ("Receive these writings, which I have composed with
          humble heart for you, good king" — trans. Stockton).

51–54   *Cordis amore . . . tuli.* Gesture and language here suggest the poem was a gift,
          perhaps commemorating the coronation, but more likely Henry's "election" on
          30 September 1399. Gower may have been under some pressure to write it:
          Henry, perhaps influenced by his experience in Milan at the Visconti court,
          where laudatory poetry was valued for the impression it could create, attempted
          to lure Christine de Pisan to join his service in 1399 (as did Gian Galeazzo
          Visconti, slightly later), and doubtless Gower — and Chaucer — were "encour-
          aged" as well. See Yeager, "Begging," and more broadly, Jones et al., *Who
          Murdered Chaucer?*

52   *quia.* So S, H. Mac: *qui.*

          michi. So S, H. Mac: *mihi.*

8. O RECOLENDE

Suggested as an acknowledgment for two pipes of Gascon wine awarded Gower by Henry
on 21 November 1399 (see Fisher, *John Gower*, pp. 68–69), but more likely composed for the
coronation on 13 October 1399, for which occasion its advice on how to govern shows par-
ticular pertinence. The complexity of its structure — Leonine hexameters in stanzas of seven
lines with four unisonant rhymes throughout, broken by elegiac distichs — also indicates a
special occasion. In order of composition, therefore, probably the second of the three
"laureate" poems.
The text here is based on S, read against C, H, G, and H₃.

1–7   Raby (*History of Secular Latin Poetry* 2.343) notes a formal similarity of the verse
          with "the literary atmosphere of Peter Riga and Alexander Neckham," from
          both of whose works Gower frequently borrows lines to use centonically. On
          Gower's use of cento, see Yeager, "Did Gower Write Cento?"

2   *Pharaone.* Compare Exodus 1–14. The allusion to Henry IV as Moses (and thus
          here Richard II as pharaoh) continues a typological association of Henry with
          Christ begun in *Rex celi deus*; see notes to lines 12, 17–18 in that poem, above.

4   *Regni persone.* An odd recommendation, considering Henry's vow to be ruled by
          appropriate counsel, and the central charge against Richard II that "He seyd
          opynly, with a sterne chere and ouertwert, that his lawes weren in his mouthe,
          and other while in his breste, And that he allone myht chaunge the Lawes off his
          Rewme and make newe" (*Chronicles of London*, p. 31). More likely Gower has in
          mind here that Henry (in contrast to Richard who, in the habit of tyrants, was
          portrayed as whimsical and erratic) should maintain rational moderation in his
          personal affairs, as an example to all. Some additional awkwardness no doubt
          springs from the demand on *persone* to carry the difficult rhyming pattern.

5   *Pacem compone.* See note to *Rex celi deus,* line 39, above.

8   *Rex confirmatus, licet.* Obviously issues of large import to a usurper; references undoubtedly to Henry's "parliamentary election" 30 September 1399.

9   *Sub Cristo . . . inmaculatus.* Equally, if not more, significant was the issue of Henry's supplanting Richard, a ruler anointed and chosen by God. Henry's apparent concerns over his "maculate" action prompted his vows to make pilgrimage to Jerusalem and to lead a crusade, both of which his turbulent kingdom and ill health (also reckoned God's judgment, apparently by Henry himself: see Kirby, *Henry IV,* p. 256) ultimately prevented. See further *H. aquile pullus,* below.

10–11   *Est . . . moderatus.* The two parts of the complete main verb here enclose all of the social classes Gower calls to be restrained by law; a similar construction is used in line 1 of Virgil's first *Eclogue.*

14   *ad omne latus.* A contrast to Richard, whom Lancastrian writers portray as autocratic and secretive.

15–19   *pie / pietas / pius / pietatis.* Gower applies similar designations to Henry at the end of *Cronica* (III.462–73); they are here translated as forms of "mercy," following Macaulay (4.415–16):

> The epithet "pius," which Gower attaches to Henry's name in this passage, means in his mouth "merciful," and in the margin [of S] the "pietas" of the new king is contrasted with the "cruelty" of Richard, the vice to which Gower chiefly attributes his fall. There is no doubt that the execution of Arundel and the murder of Gloucester (or the popular opinion that he had been murdered) produced a very sinister impression, and caused a general feeling of insecurity which was very favourable to Henry's enterprise.

It is clear, however, that a traditional translation as "dutiful in belief" would apply equally well in the passage, and to Henry himself. See note to line 21, below.

17–21   *Qui bene . . . bibit.* These lines are written over erasure in S, C, and G. H and H₃ read:

> Dum pia vota bibit, tua fama satire nequibit,
> Plena set exhibit, cum laudeque plena redibit:
> Non sic transibit, vbicumque tirannus abibit;
> Cum nimis ascribit sibi magna, minora subibit;
> Vt meritum querit, sors sua fata gerit.

> [Whenever one drinks with a solemn vow, he cannot thirst for popular opinion,
> But will show himself satisfied, when he fully attains glory:
> Not thus it happens, whenever a tyrant dies;
> When he makes great claims for himself, he departs smaller by half;
> Wherever merit is questionable, chance determines a man's fate.]

17   *Qui bene describit . . . subibit.* Proverbial: "Know thyself;" see Whiting, K100.

18   *Set pius . . . redibit.* Proverbial (Whiting, M510); compare Matthew 5:7: "beati misericordes quia ipsi misericordiam consequentur" ("Blessed are the merciful: for they shall obtain mercy").

20   *Deus ascribit.* On God the bookkeeper, compare Apocalypse 3:5: "non delebo nomen eius de libro vitae" ("I will not blot out his name out of the book of life"), and also Apocalypse 13:8. That God will help the elect and keep them safe is proverbial (Whiting, G211), based in part on John 6:35–40.

20   *ab hoste perire nequibit.* Following *O recolende* in Tr are written lines from two Psalms: Vulgate Psalm 88:23: "Nichil proficiet inimicus in eo, et filius iniquitatis non apponet nocere ei" ("The enemy shall have no advantage over him: nor the son of iniquity have power to hurt him"); and Vulgate Psalm 40:3: "Dominus conseruet eum, et viuificet eum, et beatum faciat eum in terra, et non tradat eum in animam inimicorum eius" ("The Lord preserve him and give him life, and make him blessed upon the earth: and deliver him not up to the will of his enemies"). In G, H, and H₃ these passages follow *H. aquile pullus*; see below.

21   *pia.* So Mac, emending from C, H, G, and H₃. S: *pita.* Here translated as "mercy."

           pia vota bibit. Compare Numbers 6:1–21, describing the process of purification leading to consecration and sanctification: "Ista est lex nazaraei, cum voverit oblationem suam Domino tempore consecrationis suae, exceptis his, quae invenerit manus eius: iuxta quod mente devoverat, ita faciet ad perfectionem sanctificationis suae" ("This is the law of the Nazarite, when he hath vowed his oblation to the Lord in the time of his consecration. Besides those things which his hand shall find according to that which he had vowed in his mind, so shall he do for the fulfilling of his sanctification"). Immediately follows (6:24–27) the Lord's blessing for Moses and Aaron, promising mercy, protection, and peace.

9. H. AQUILE PULLUS

Conceivably the last written of the "laureate" poems; perhaps (as suggested by Fisher, *John Gower*, p. 99) intended for the coronation, 13 October 1399, but more probably the stanza addresses the elevation of the future Henry V to Prince of Wales on 15 October, or his creation as duke of Aquitaine on the twenty-third — or (most likely) both. Resembling the prophecy they render, the four lines culminate in a reference to the prince; nor would Gower likely have known of the "oleum" (Richard having kept it on his person) prior to the coronation, when it was used ostentatiously to anoint Henry IV, by way of countering publicly Richard's sacral kingship. See *O recolende*, note to line 9, above.

In three MSS (G, H, and H₃), these four lines follow *Cronica* and are themselves followed by two quotations from the Bible: Vulgate Psalm 88:23 ("Nichil proficiet inimicus in eo, et filius iniquitatis non apponet nocere ei" ["The enemy shall have no advantage over him: nor the son of iniquity have power to hurt him"]) and Vulgate Psalm 40:3 ("Dominus conseruet eum, et viuificet eum, et beatum faciat eum in terra, et non tradat eum in animam inimicorum eius" ["The Lord preserve him and give him life, and make him blessed upon the earth: and deliver him not up to the will of his enemies"]). In Tr, however, these lines are attached to the end of *O recolende*, itself used to introduce *CB*. In the remaining manuscripts, the poem appears independent of direct association with another work.

H. aquile pullus is written in Leonine hexameter; the text presented here is based on S. Other versions survive in C, H, G, H₃, and Tr.

1 *H. aquile pullus.* Beside this line, the scribe of S has entered the word *Prophecia* ("Prophecy") in the margin. It is likely more than one prophecy was intended, as the poem makes reference to two. Here the reference is to the "Prophecy of the Eagle," a thirteenth-century offshoot of the Merlin prophecies (compare Geoffrey of Monmouth's *Historia Regum Britannie* VII), which among Lancastrian supporters associated Henry IV with an eaglet (*pullus aquilae*) who comes from across the sea to depose a white king (*rex albus* — i.e., Richard, whose badge was a white hart). Henry was supposed the eagle because the symbol of John the Evangelist, namesake of his father, John of Gaunt, was an eagle, and because the badge of Edward III, his grandfather, was an eagle also — little notice was given to Edward's status as Richard's grandfather also. The association of Henry as an eagle became quite common in the early fifteenth century; see, for example, *Richard the Redeless* 2.9. Compare Macaulay 4.416 and Usk, *Chronicon*, pp. 50–53. Prophecy was a part of the Lancastrian propaganda effort to substantiate their claims to the crown: see Strohm, *England's Empty Throne*, pp.1–31.

2 *colla.* So Mac, emending from C, H, H₃, and Tr. S: *bella.* As Macaulay notes (4.416), however, the S reading seems to be working from *VC* VI.xii.876, "where our author in borrowing from the *Aurora* substitutes 'bella' for 'corda' or 'colla.'"

3 *H. aquile.* Henry of Grosmont, first duke of Lancaster, who, legend had it, "captured" the oil (*oleum*) in France and gave it to Edward the Black Prince for use in his coronation.

   oleum. A legendary and prophetic oil, given first to Thomas à Becket by the Virgin Mary during his exile in France. Intended to anoint a future king who would, without bloodshed, recover England and the lost Aquitaine, the oil was purportedly left in the Tower by the Black Prince, where Richard discovered it too late for his own anointing — although he did approach Archbishop Thomas Arundel about a second ceremony, but was rebuffed. See note to line 2, above, McKenna, "Coronation Oil," and Saul, *Richard II*, pp. 423–24.

4 *Sic veteri . . . uncta.* Compare *Cronica* III.352–55, where the allusion is to Prince Henry, Gower's passage describing the ceremony confirming him as Prince of Wales on 15 October 1399:

   Henrici natus Henricus, honore beatus,
   Est confirmatus heres Princepsque vocatus:
   Sic pars abscissa, summo de iudice visa,
   Arboris est vncta veteri stipitque reiuncta.

   (Henry the son of Henry was confirmed as heir and named Prince. Thus the part of the tree which had been cut off was anointed in the sight of the highest Judge and rejoined to its former trunk — trans. Stockton.)

10. QUICQUID HOMO SCRIBAT (IN FINE)

This poem — or is it three? — survives in three versions in five manuscripts: S, C (also surviving in H and G), and Tr versions. Tr and C are sufficiently different from S — which alone begins *Quicquid homo scribat* — that they are sometimes identified as *In fine*, the title being taken from the prose note which accompanies the version in C. (But since a nearly identical prose note appears in S, but not in Tr, which lacks a note altogether, *In fine* as a title for Tr and C would seem only to add to the confusion.) Macaulay posited S as the "final" version because Gower included it in the manuscript presented to Archbishop Arundel ca. 1402 or later, and for this reason grouped all three under a single title derived from the (unique) first line of S — a choice with complications of its own, as one can search in vain for those words in the texts of Tr and C. In support of Macaulay's ordering are statements in Tr and C that they were composed in 1400 and 1401, respectively (i.e., the first and second year of Henry IV's reign). The difficulty proceeds from the relationship of the three versions: Tr and C are the closest to each other, while S shares lines, phrases and words with both, an additional factor pointing toward S as the latest version. However, commonalities between S and Tr, and S and C, are not shared by Tr and C: Gower, it would appear, had either copies of, or memory of, both Tr and C available when he wrote S, and drew on both. *Quicquid homo scribat* is retained here as a title for all three, in deference to the familiarity of Macaulay's edition.

That there are three versions of what Stockton (*Major Latin Works*, p. 36) has called "Gower's farewell to writing" lacks neither interest nor irony. Despite his protests of lost eyesight, Gower seems to have kept writing, indicating perhaps some latitude in what he meant by his "blindness" (a claim, after all, discoverable in his work for some years) and consequent inability to write. The question of whether age and blindness were a conscious pose for literary purposes is raised by Yeager ("Gower in Winter"). All three versions are in elegiac distichs, rhyming erratically and possibly coincidentally, the second version (at line 15) and the third (at line 17) with unusual pentameters (see Carlson, "Rhyme").

[All Souls version]

2   *velud.* So S. Mac reads *velut.*

11   *Quamuis exterius.* Mac reads *Quamuis ad exterius,* but *ad* is clearly marked for deletion in the MS.

11. PRESUL OUILE REGIS

If a note in the margin of C (see note to lines 1 ff., below) is accurate regarding its subject, then the poem can be dated 1402, the year a great comet was visible across England and the Continent, universally interpreted as presaging disaster. Adam Usk, for example, thought it foretold the death of Gian Galeazzo Visconti, duke of Milan (*Chronicle*, p. 155). Macaulay (4.420) takes *Presul* as written for Archbishop Arundel. The text is from C, read against H and G. The form is intricate: three Leonine hexameter couplets with disyllabic collateral rhyme in "-egis" and "-arum" throughout, concluding with an elegiac distich, both disyllabic rhymes being "-arum."

1 ff.   ☞ **Latin marginalia** in C: *Nota de primordiis Stelle Comate in Anglia*. ["Note on the comet in England"]

1   *morbus . . . macularum.* Gower commonly equates heresy with the plague: compare *CVP*, note to line 11 and *O deus immense*, line 31, both above; and *Unanimes esse qui secula*, note to line 6, below.

2   *pestis.* See preceding note.

4   *insidiarum.* Henry's early reign was rife with plots on his life, real and imagined. In 1402, in addition to the Welsh insurrection of Owain Glendower, conspiracies to kill Henry by Sir Roger Clarendon (a bastard son of the Black Prince) and the Austin prior of Launde were put down, as was another hatched by the Franciscans of Winchelsea, up to a dozen of whom Usk reports (*Chronicle*, p. 175) may have been executed.

12. UNANIMES ESSE QUI SECULA

Also probably datable ca. 1402, although on slim evidence. In the manuscripts it occurs between *Presul* and *Orate pro anima*, a poem likely very late, perhaps ca. 1408, when Gower died. If "heri" in line 7 can be taken as a reference to Richard II's reign, and at roughly face value, it may denote a date of composition not long after Henry IV took power. The structure is unisonant hexameter couplets exhibiting five disyllabic rhymes, with the final line an elegiac distich.

The text here is based on C, read against H, G, and E.

1–2   *Unanimes . . . amor superesse.* The opening echoes Boethius: compare *De cons.* 3.met.9 and 2.met.8.

6   *errorem quasi pestis.* Gower often depicts heresy as plague; see *Presul*, note to line 1, above.

13. CULTOR IN ECCLESIA

In the manuscripts, inscribed after *Presul* but before *Dicunt scripture* — hence a composition date of 1402–08 is perhaps as close as can be surmised safely. Seemingly addressing a topical situation, the conclusions — and the corruptions cited — are general enough to be applicable at almost any point in Gower's lifetime. (Indeed, they would be comfortable addressed to the church under Richard II, rather than under a restored Archbishop Arundel, whose authority Gower clearly respected.) The form is Leonines with disyllabic rhyme, lines 1–6 in elegiac distichs, 7–12 in hexameters.

The text here is based on C, read against H, G, and E.

1–6   *Cultor . . . serat.* Compare Matthew 21:33–44, the Parable of the Husbandmen, and 13:3–30, those of the Sower and of the Good Seed and the Tares.

8   *Symon.* Simon Magus; see *De lucis scrutinio*, note to line 8, above.

9   *Querat . . . sine crimine puram.* Compare John 8:7: "qui sine peccato est vestrum primus in illam lapidem mittat" ("He that is without sin among you, let him cast the first stone").

14. DICUNT SCRIPTURE

Perhaps written in conjunction with his will, produced 15 August 1408 and proved 24 October of the same year. See Macaulay 4.xvii; the will is reproduced in translation on 4.xvii–xviii. The form is Leonine elegiac distichs, each line with a separate monosyllabic rhyme.

The text here is from C, read against H, G, and E.

1 ff.	☞ **Latin marginalia** in C: *Nota contra mortuorum executors*. ["Note against the executors of death."]
1	*novissima vite*. Undoubtedly intended are the "Four Last Things," i.e., death, judgment, hell, and heaven, which are not scriptural (although thought to be adapted from Paul: compare Hebrews 6:2, 9:27) but traditional or proverbial. See *CVP*, Marginalia to lines 302 ff.
6	*sis memor ergo tue*. Perhaps reflecting the care Gower took to create his own monument — the tomb with its lifelike effigy at St. Mary Overys, its head resting on his three major books; the carefully spelled-out will; provision included there for daily masses for his soul, and an obit sung annually (according to Berthelette, in the preface to his 1532 edition of the *Confessio Amantis*, quoted in Mac 4.420) "on fryday after the feaste of the blessed pope saynte Gregory." Apparently Gower provided for a monument of some sort for Agnes as well, but nothing of it now remains, nor is a physical description known (although John Bale records an epitaph, presumably attached; see Mac 4.lix, and Hines, Cohen, and Roffey, "*Johannes Gower, Armiger, Poeta*," p. 27).

15. ORATE PRO ANIMA (ARMIGERI SCUTUM)

Intended as an epitaph (once inscribed on his tomb, it is no longer visible), it seems likely from the same period and impulse as *Dicunt scripture* — i.e., early fall of 1408. Macaulay (4.420) calls attention to *CVP*, lines 217–24, as a passage similar in style and sentiment. The prose text survives in two distinct versions: C (also surviving in H) and G versions, with the C version probably being the older of the two; the poem itself only appears in G. The form is Leonine hexameters rhyming unisontantly eight times in "-utum."

In G a sketch of two angels holding a shield bearing three lion heads in a chevron is included between the heading and the poem — presumably Gower's arms. (See Fisher, *John Gower*, pp. 37–39, and Figure 1.) A similar shield now hangs above his tomb in Southwark Cathedral (see Fisher, *John Gower*, Figure 2). A drawing of a bier, with candles at head and foot, follows the poem, suggesting G's completion after Gower's death.

Glasgow version

2	*Reddidit immo lutum*. Compare Genesis 3:19, and *CVP*, note to lines 218–19, above.

◈ Appendix 1: Eneidos bucolis

Macaulay printed *Eneidos bucolis* among Gower's Latin works, between *Quia unusquisque* and *O deus immense*, even as he surmised their author to have been "Ralph Strode, whom Chaucer couples with Gower in the last stanza of *Troilus* with the epithet 'philosophical,' and of whom we know by tradition that he wrote elegiac verse" (4.419). Precisely why Macaulay chose to hold out Gower's own authorship through this inclusion, without comment, in the text, only to reverse himself in the notes, is a small mystery. If, however, the unusual editorial maneuver indicates ambivalence on Macaulay's part as to Gower's hand in the poem, he is not alone. There is a case to be made that *Eneidos bucolis*, which appears in five manuscripts (including two that Gower may have overseen in production, S and F), could indeed be Gower's own effort. Its form is elegiac couplets, of which he was a master; nor would it be the first or only time that he adopted a "philosophical" detachment to comment on himself in the third person. The chapter headings in *VC* (e.g., "In huius opusculi principio intendit compositor" ["In the beginning of this little work the author intends"]), the address/prayer prefacing the dedication of S to Archbishop Arundel (e.g., "Hanc Epistolam subscriptam corde deuoto misit senex et cecus Iohannes Gower" ["This Epistle, written with a devoted heart, the old and blind John Gower has sent"]) come to mind; and, although their level of invention is less than creating an alterego to praise one's own achievement, the Latin note at *CA* I.60 ff., "fingens se auctor esse Amantem" ["the author feigning to be the Lover"], strikes closer. Amans, it has long been recognized, both is, and is not, the "John Gower" he eventually claims to be at *CA* VIII.2908. If *Eneidos bucolis* is by Gower, it presents an advance on his demonstrated fictive self-fashioning, but not an inconceivable one; and it would tell us much about how he wished to situate himself *memoria in aeterna*.

On the other hand, if it is, in fact, by someone else, its quintuple presence in manuscripts of his work may indicate how well Gower thought *Eneidos bucolis* caught his likeness.

The text here is from S, collated with C, H, G, and F. The form is elegiac distichs.

ENEIDOS BUCOLIS

Carmen, quod quidam Philosophus in memoriam Iohannis Gower super consum-
macione suorum trium librorum forma subsequenti composuit, et eidem gratanter
transmisit.

> *Eneidos*, *Bucolis*, que *Georgica* metra perhennis
>   Virgilio laudis serta dedere scolis;
> Hiis tribus ille libris prefertur honore poetis,
>   Romaque precipuis laudibus instat eis.
5 Gower, sicque tuis tribus est dotata libellis
>   Anglia, morigeris quo tua scripta seris.
> Illeque Latinis tantum sua metra loquelis
>   Scripsit, ut Italicis sint recolenda notis;
> Te tua set trinis tria scribere carmina linguis
10   Constat, ut inde viris sit scola lata magis:
> Gallica lingua prius, Latina secunda, set ortus
>   Lingua tui pocius Anglica complet opus.
> Ille quidem vanis Romanas obstupet aures,
>   Ludit et in studiis musa pagana suis;
15 Set tua Cristicolis fulget scriptura renatis,
>   Quo tibi celicolis laus sit habenda locis.

AENEID BUCOLICS

A poem, which in remembrance of John Gower a certain philosopher composed in the following form and happily sent to the same man, to commemorate the completion of his three books.

The meters of the *Aeneid*, *Bucolics*, and *Georgics*, woven together
    By Virgil, have given matter of perennial praise to the schools.
On account of these three books he is preferred in honor over all poets,
    And Rome bestows upon them its chief praises.
5   Thus, too, O Gower, with your three little books is England endowed,
    Where you accommodate your writings to serious things.
He wrote his poems only in the Latin tongue,
    So that they might be appreciated by the famous Italian worthies.
But it is clear that you wrote your three poems in three languages,
10   So that broader schooling might be given to men.
First the French tongue, Latin second, then at last English,
    The speech of your birth, completes the work.
He indeed astounded the ears of the Romans with vanities,
    And the pagan Muse played in his studies.
15   But your writing glows for reborn Christians,
    Whereby praise will be given you in heavenly places.

NOTES TO *ENEIDOS BUCOLIS*

Prose   *Philosophus.* An alternative translation could be the more general "wise man," with implications for the identity of "philosophical" Strode; on whom see Delasanta, "Chaucer and Strode." Macaulay (4.419) suggests this *Philosophus* as also the author of a quatrain following *CA* in many manuscripts including F, prefaced by the heading "Epistola super huius opusculi sui complementum Iohanni Gower a quodam philosopho transmissa" ("A letter about the completion of this, his little work, sent to John Gower by a certain philosopher"):

> Quam cinxere freta Gower tua carmina leta
> Per loca discreta canit Anglia laude repleta.
> Carminis Athleta satirus tibi sive Poeta
> Sit laus completa quo gloria stat sine meta.

> [O Gower, enclosed by the sea and filled with praise
> England, throughout many regions, recites your joyous poetry.
> Master of verse, satirist — or poet — for you
> May praise be full where glory stands without end.]

1   *Eneidos, Bucolis, que Georgica.* Although Gower's work makes infrequent direct use of Virgil, and his reading beyond the *Aeneid* must remain in doubt, that he knew Virgil's oeuvre by name seems incontestable. In the same manner he would have been aware of Virgil's achievement, sufficient to recognize it as a writer's model and to pay himself — or accept — a high compliment with the comparison.

5   *libellis.* "Little books," compared to Virgil's "libris" (line 3). The humility topos is standard. Compare Chaucer's "Go litel bok" (*TC* 5.1786) and the concluding stanzas of *Troilus* generally, with which classicizing sensibility (and competitive self-assertion) *Eneidos bucolis* has much in common.

In Praise of Peace

INTRODUCTION

John Gower wrote two known works in English.[1] The first, and certainly the more famous, is his monumental *Confessio Amantis*. The second is a far shorter poem called *In Praise of Peace*.[2] John Fisher argued that the latter was, in fact, "Gower's last important poem. It sums up the final twenty years of both his literary career and his literary achievement. The former is obsessed with the king, the latter with the idea of kingship."[3] Whether or not one agrees with Fisher's assessment of the relative importance of Gower's later Latin works, many of which postdate *In Praise of Peace*, he is quite right in seeing this poem as an enchiridion of sorts, a recapitulation of the most pervasive themes of Gower's many works. Written in late 1399 or early 1400 on the occasion of Henry IV's rise to the throne,[4] *In Praise of Peace* once more places Gower in what George Coffman has called his "most significant role": that of advisor to the king on the nature of right rule.[5] To that end, Gower's advice would seem simple enough. As Masayoshi Itô summarizes:

---

[1] Thanks must go to R. F. Yeager for allowing me to participate so thoroughly in the construction of this volume. He is a generous man, and one to whom all scholars of Middle English owe a great debt: without him our knowledge of Gower, and, in turn, of late medieval England, would be far from that which we enjoy today. Thanks also are due to Russell A. Peck, general editor of the series, who first proposed that this volume be undertaken; it was his constant encouragement and gentle correction that helped speed both of us along.

[2] The poem is not titled in the sole surviving manuscript copy. As Macaulay observes (3.553), Skeat called the work *The Praise of Peace*, whereas he himself titles it *To King Henry the Fourth in Praise of Peace*. Most modern critics, however, have abbreviated Macaulay's title to the more simple *In Praise of Peace*.

[3] Fisher, *John Gower*, p. 133.

[4] For overall discussion of Henry's conquest, see Bennett, "Henry of Bolingbroke and the Revolution of 1399." Strohm has suggested that the poem could date from as late as 1404 (*Hochon's Arrow*, p. 90), but this seems unlikely. Grady notes that "the poem's opening movement concludes with a hymn to national unity that, given the disturbances of the early years of the reign, must have seemed like rhetorical excess any time after October 1399" ("Lancastrian Gower," p. 560). The call to peace would certainly have been a more difficult "sell" after the Epiphany Rising in the following January, much less subsequent to the Franciscan plots of 1402 or the Percys' Revolt of summer 1403 (for discussion of the latter, see Neville, "Scotland, the Percies and the Law in 1400"; Arvanigian, "Henry IV, the Northern Nobility and the Consolidation of the Regime"; and King, "'They have the Hertes of the People by North'"). In addition to these contexts, Gower's reference to a papal bull directing Christendom against the "pagans" (lines 208–10) also argues strongly for 1399–1400 as the likely date of composition (see the explanatory note to line 208).

[5] See Coffman, "John Gower in His Most Significant Role." For additional context of Gower as a poet involved in politics, see Green, *Poets and Princepleasers*, especially pp. 179–83.

It is a political poem in which Gower, as a loyal subject of Henry IV, approves his coronation, admires him as the saviour of England, dilates on the evil of war and the blessing of peace, and finally begs him to display clemency and seek domestic peace. . . . [H]e is asking Henry IV to apply a new policy of peace to the body politic — England — which has weakened in the long war against France.[6]

Along the way, as Fisher shows in his own brief synopsis of the poem, Gower addresses "the parliamentary proceedings leading to Henry's accession," posits that "the Schism is the main cause of war between and within nations," and asserts "the superiority of civil to canon law."[7] Gower's recurring praise in the poem of not just peace, but the person of the king himself, led Paul Strohm to consider it simply a piece of Lancastrian propaganda.[8] And the poem's place as an English capstone to a career of writing for, to, and about England's princes brought Fisher to the point of questioning whether there has "ever been a greater sycophant in the history of English literature" than Gower.[9] The simplistic reductions of such observations has left *In Praise of Peace* in the same position as the shorter Latin works edited and translated in this volume: ignored, neglected, reduced, or relegated to the dusty realm of footnotes. But there is far more at work in this complex poem, as Gower's verse deftly weaves in and out of the historical, political, social, and religious contexts and controversies of its day. Even when he refuses to name names, Gower is always topical.

IN PRAISE OF PEACE AND THE *CONFESSIO AMANTIS*

In Praise of Peace is written in rhyme royal, the same verse form that Gower used for Amans' prayer to Venus at the end of the *Confessio Amantis* (8.2217–2300),[10] and this formal, stylistic echo points to deeper thematic and imaginative continuities between Gower's two English poems. Near the conclusion of the earlier work, after Venus has replied favorably to Amans' supplication and is preparing to take her leave from the newly identified and reunified "John Gower," the goddess gives the aging poet a last set of instructions:

Mi sone, be wel war therfore,	*well advised*
And kep the sentence of my lore	*teaching*
And tarie thou mi court no more,	
Bot go ther vertu moral duelleth,	*where*
Wher ben thi bokes, as men telleth,	
Whiche of long time thou hast write. (*CA* 8.2922–27)	

---

[6] Itô, *John Gower*, p. 106.

[7] Fisher, *John Gower*, pp. 132–33.

[8] Strohm, *Hochon's Arrow*, pp. 75–94.

[9] Fisher, *John Gower*, p. 133. Such comment might remind us of Spenser, whom Karl Marx derided as Elizabeth's "arse-kissing poet": without denying that there is some element of truth to the fact of Spenser's loyalty to royalty, scholars have increasingly noted the often subtle subtexts to his work in which the poet looks to "tutor his queen" and "impress in her princely mind the confused misery which, because of her benevolence, corrupts her Irish colony" (Baker, *Between Nations*, p. 115; see also Bates, "'The Queene is Defrauded of the Intent of the Law,'" especially pp. 123–25). Gower, too, has been redeemed from later scholarship's not-wholly-accurate depictions of him as a sycophant.

[10] For comparison between these two works in their stanzaic forms, see Itô, *John Gower*, pp. 101–17.

Forced from the court of Love, Gower is instructed to return to the books he has so long labored over, books where moral virtues can be found. Venus calls for a revisitation of the past as a present connection to the future; she asks him, as it were, to try it all over again.[11] We know that Gower was not averse to altering the *Confessio* — nowhere is this more clearly attested to than in his revisions to the prologue and conclusion as he moves from a Ricardian to a Lancastrian recension — but we can see, too, that Venus' order is directed at more than just revisions of the *Confessio*: many of Gower's writings after the "completion" of his English *magnum opus* revolve around the recasting of themes from his earlier works. This recasting process can be not only thematic in theory, but also literal in practice as Gower at times recycles specific lines from one poem into another. Even so, we must be careful not to view such recapitulations, whether general or particular, as signs of laziness or lack of imagination on the part of the poet; to the contrary, they are renewals of purpose that reveal a remarkable continuity of thinking on Gower's part. When Venus asks the poet to begin again, she does not say whether she expects him necessarily to come to a different conclusion. Indeed, the unidirectional nature of time would dictate, for instance, that the ending of the *Confessio*, with its stark realization of age and natural incapacities, is the only ending that could ever be reached. The poet's refashioning is thus predetermined, dictated by the original delineation of the poem (of its creation, we might say) not because Gower refuses to change his mind but because, since nothing could be more deliberate than the natural state of the poet's mind, time invariably has its way.

Book 3 of the *Confessio* is devoted to Wrath, which stands against the virtues of patience and mercy. Foremost among this vice's guises, Genius explains, is Homicide — not only a vice but a mortal sin. As his first exemplum to warn Amans about the danger of Homicide, Genius uses the Tale of Alexander and the Pirate, in which Alexander is repeatedly termed a tyrant and which reveals the difference between the rogue and the conqueror as one of semantics.[12] At the conclusion of the tale Genius admits that Alexander had success for a time, but he is also quick to point out the bleak end of his life:

And as he hath the world mistimed	
Noght as he scholde with his wit,	
Noght as he wolde it was aquit.	*repaid*
Thus was he slain that whilom slowh,	*slew*
And he which riche was ynowh	
This dai, tomorwe he hadde noght.	*nothing*
And in such wise as he hath wroght	
In destorbance of worldes pes,	*peace*
His werre he fond thanne endeles,	*war*
In which forevere desconfit	*vanquished*
He was. (*CA* 3.2458–68)	

---

[11] The full implications of this philosophical framework, whereby understanding is only approached (but never achieved) through constant revision of life and work, cannot be fully explicated here. I hope, however, to explore them more fully in a future work comparing Gower and the other famous habitual reviser of late medieval England, William Langland.

[12] Alexander's other major tale in the *Confessio*, the Tale of Diogenes and Alexander, is also unflattering to the conqueror, being told by Genius only a little earlier in Book 3 as an example of Contek (Discord), another of Wrath's guises; see *CA* 3.1089–1328.

Gower presents Alexander as a man for whom endless war — the consequence of mistimed judgments — is a kind of piracy that destroys both the state and the graces of peace.

Despite such a warning, the possibility that the newly crowned Henry might long to follow Alexander in conquest was apparently very much in the air as Gower is writing *In Praise of Peace*: Frank Grady points out that Jean Creton, in his *Histoire du Roy d'Angleterre Richard*, "describes how the 'simple and over-credulous' commons, impressed with 'how that he had conquered the whole kingdom of England in less than a month,' 'said, that he would conquer one of the great portions of the world, and compared him even to Alexander the Great'" ("Lancastrian Gower," p. 564). Gower's subsequent use of Alexander in his new poem as a model to be feared rather than followed is intimately tied, no doubt, to what Gower perceived as the threat of such aspirations. Alexander, for Gower, had never been a model worthy of emulation, and Henry's successes, though real, did not change that opinion.[13] Gower gives every indication that he expects Henry to be aware of the corresponding treatments of his subject in the *Confessio* and *In Praise of Peace*, and, indeed, Gower goes some way toward underscoring the correlation between the poems by adapting for the central argument of *In Praise of Peace* numerous lines from Genius' lecture against Homicide and war — especially those lines immediately preceding the Tale of Alexander and the Pirate.[14] The literal refashioning of lines, which even extends to Gower's Latin works, corresponds to the general recapitulation of his career in this poem, and reveals various levels at which Gower's revisionary process unfolds. We are able to see, thereby, that the poet's comments against war and killing in Book 3 of the *Confessio*, for example, were never to be understood as definitive: they were perpetual, ever-renewed and ever-renewing.

Gower never views time in a static way. Quite to the contrary, he follows Augustine who, in his own *Confessio*, had pronounced the present moment to be an immeasurable, transitive, and essentially non-existent illusion, created within the mind of memory as it struggles to conceive of itself between an imagined past and a potential future.[15] Augustine's famous example for this concept is the reciting of a psalm, an act through which he is able to bridge past and future, effectively building a temporal, if temporary, present.[16] Gower announces his own debt to these Augustinian principles in his massive Latin poem *Vox Clamantis*, which he begins with the lines "Scripture veteris capiunt exempla futuri, / Nam dabit experta res magis esse fidem" ["Old writings hold examples for the future, / For a thing put to the test will grant greater faith"].[17] Reading, as it presents the past within the moment, is the perpetual key to comprehension. In the face of the monstrous chaos of time, which, like the mind that perceives it, is perpetually being reinvented by its own passing in the same way that a rock rolling down a

---

[13] This conclusion goes against that reached by Grady, who accuses Gower of being "incapable of condemning Alexander" ("Lancastrian Gower," p. 563); for more, see the explanatory notes to lines 36–42 and 45.

[14] A reading of the explanatory notes that here follow the poem will provide some notion of the many ties between *In Praise of Peace* and the *Confessio*, but see especially the notes to lines 24–25, 29–35, 36–42, 45, 78, 95, 107–08, 113, 115, 122, 155, 250, 337–57, and 365–66.

[15] *Confessions* 11.15.20. For discussion of similarities between Augustine and Gower on time, see Gower's *Confessio Amantis*, ed. Peck, 1.1–5.

[16] *Confessions* 11.28.38.

[17] Gower, *Vox Clamantis*, ed. Macaulay, 4.20 (Prol. to Book I, lines 1–2); trans. my own.

mountain alters both itself and the slope on which it moves,[18] all man can do is to try and grip the present, futile task though it must be, by crafting stories of his past.[19] And if those stories are the key to our comprehending both past and our constantly reconceived present, they are thus the key to our preparing for the future. All is dependent, it seems, on right reading of our own invented fictions. As Russell A. Peck states the matter, "Gower enters into a refined phenomenology where time, history, memory, and a fictionalizing of the past make discourse of the 'now'-world presentable."[20] The poet's rewritings thus reassert a single-minded agenda and vision, a philosophy of logic in the face of chaos that, as we will see, Gower builds structurally into *In Praise of Peace* so that we might more easily comprehend its message of rational morality. Gower's poetics, in other words, are always textual.[21]

THE POEM AND ITS STRUCTURE

Writing for Henry IV shortly after (or perhaps on the very occasion of) his coronation, Gower could not be faulted if he were to have regarded *In Praise of Peace* as the final movement in his long, often tragic literary symphony that honored his homeland even as it lamented so much of what had befallen it. With the new dawn of Henry's rule, Gower's voice would no longer be a voice on the outside, one crying out in the wilderness and resolutely exposing the moral desolation of his age. Now his could be a voice on the inside, one directly guiding the ruler of his country and gently correcting that desolation. The hope that he had held for England despite all of its travails — a battered but defiant hope that is probably most clearly expressed in the prayer for England at the end of the Lancastrian "third recension" of his *Confessio* — had been fulfilled. Times *were* changing. In the *Cronica Tripertita* Gower had outlined the many iniquities and perversions of right during Richard's reign that called out for intervention, and that intervention had come in the form of Henry, who had stepped into the breach first to claim what was rightfully his, then to restore proper law whereby all England might once again live in mutual productivity. The tone of the successive *In Praise of Peace* is, if not triumphant, determinedly optimistic. In this light, we might view the poem as a coda to Gower's long career, restating and reinvigorating his famously moral principles about just rule of self and society.

Gower sets forth the essence of the principles he will expound in the Latin proem that introduces *In Praise of Peace*. Like so much of his Latin work, this seven-line epigram is meticulously crafted, setting a careful tone for the vernacular work that follows it. Beginning with

---

[18] The parallel, of course, is to Nebuchadnezzar's dream of the monster of time and the rolling, seemingly heedless stone that smashes it, both of which feature prominently in the text of the Prologue of the *Confessio*, lines 585 ff., and in many of its accompanying manuscript illuminations. For examples of these images, see Gower, *Confessio Amantis*, ed. Peck, vol. 1, figs. 2 and 4.

[19] "Time is thus a kind of fiction — a tale, if you will — a distension of once-upon-a-time moments, stretching feeling according to measures made 'real' as the mind expands itself through anticipation of the future and recollection of the past. . . . We make tales of time through which we imagine that we can grasp its being" (Gower, *Confessio Amantis*, ed. Peck, vol. 1, p. 3n8, paraphrasing Augustine's *Confessions* 11.31.41).

[20] Gower, *Confessio Amantis*, ed. Peck, vol. 1, p. 5.

[21] Peck makes a similar claim in "John Gower: Editor," where he illustrates the "edited" quality of the *Confessio* and its ramifications for Gower's pedagogical style.

commendation for Henry's assumption to the throne, its first words, "Electus Cristi," speak volumes. Henry is Christ's elect, His chosen keeper of the throne of England. Such a commendation glorifies Henry, of course, signifying a "divine right" to his kingship, and it simultaneously places Henry into a more passive role than his armed conquest might otherwise attest — the latter "passivication" paralleling the pacification Gower will counsel throughout the poem that follows. But there is another, perhaps sharper, edge implied in such a start. Placing Christ at the beginning of his poem is a call for humility. Not only is it a reminder of Christ's own humility, but it is also a reminder that, even at the zenith of his fortunes and power, Henry must recognize a greater authority who as Word was God in Creation: the secular rights of the king are ultimately subservient to the sacred rights of divinity.[22] Gower's subsequent phrase in the Latin underlines this very point, as he characterizes the king as "pie Rex Henrice," a description that could mean respectful, dutiful, faithful, devoted, loyal, conscientious, devout, or even righteous. The next two lines of the Latin proem Henry's assumption as rightful and good; Richard's reign, by implied contrast, was evil. In the following line Gower speaks of the new joy brought to the people of England, praise not to flatter the king, but to remind him that his primary duty is to care for those very people.

The remainder of the opening proem conveys the new hope that Gower has for the land, words that remind the king of the poet's prayer for England at the end of the Henry-dedication of the *Confessio* even as the poet embarks on a new English prayer asking for the king to restore grace to the land through free and honest blessing. This Latin poem thus establishes several of the themes that run through the vernacular poem that follows: positioning of the king in relationship to Christ, praise of Henry tempered with warning counsel, and subtle reminders that rule of self must be maintained through awareness of the present and the past, both of which are best accessed through right reading at both literal and metaphoric levels. Significant, too, is the fact that he includes such a Latin proem at all. Its presence calls attention to the "Englishness" of the English poem in a way that English lines alone could never do,[23] and, at the same time, the Latin lines signify Gower's as a voice of authority, able to converse in the tongue of Antiquity and the Church even as he sets out to speak in the tongue of his homeland.

Already we can see in the opening proem how Gower's argument develops in careful, logical steps. In the 385 vernacular lines that follow, this steady process becomes even more methodological, progressing from general hypothesis to specificity through the use of particular exempla, patiently constructing a conclusion that is, or becomes, personal in application. Often the poet then tests each conclusion through suppositional logic in order to prove its general applicability. The poet's logic itself thereby informs the development of

---

[22] Here again we might note continuity with the *Confessio*, since Gower introduces Nebuchadnezzar's dream as an event that occurs under the "hyhe almyhti pourveance" of God who holds in His "eterne remembrance . . . every thing present" (*CA* Prol.585–87). In Gower's ideolect, a divine right of kingship is perhaps better termed a divine watch to kings.

[23] There is also something to be said for the fact that the Latin lines are so few in number, and so soon overtaken by the English. Though he would never again, to our knowledge, compose in English, Gower clearly felt that there was a specificity gained in addressing the new king in the vernacular. And though one hesitates to look on this as nationalism, it does have the ring of national consciousness as Gower, once the voice in the wilderness, becomes the voice of the masses. Perhaps, too, there is significance in Henry's challenge for the throne, said in English (see *Rotuli Parliamentorum* 3.422–23).

Gower's verse as he develops rational conclusions through the building of rational presentations. The poem's structure encodes its meaning, logic leading to logic.

But the lesson of logic is not the only theme that Gower embeds within the structure of this complex poem. In his *Confessio* Gower had written extensively on sin as "moder of divisioun" (Prol.1030), which itself was "moder of confusioun" (Prol.852); and there is little doubt that when he looked about England at the end of Richard's reign he saw nothing but the divisive confusion that he had so shrewdly anticipated. In that earlier work Gower had seemed to search among the poets for a new Arion to bring about peace and unity from harmful war and division (Prol.1053–77), but in this poem it is unmistakably God who, through Henry as agent-regent, addresses the division of the kingdom. Rather than becoming the new Arion, the poet is instead the peacemaker's witness and commentator, active in the process only insofar as he is able to help Henry (in this case) better understand and implement God's will — which is not to reduce the role of the poet but to make it all the more essential. And it is this theme of replacing division with unity that is also symbolized in the poem's structure. For if we are to assume authorial intention in the larger capitals that appear at the beginning of certain stanzas in the sole surviving manuscript copy of *In Praise of Peace*, the poem is divided into nine sections of varying length, to which a final stanza has been "appended" for a total of ten divisions[24] — a sum that, like the totaling of Dante's cantos in the *Commedia* ($1+33+33+33 = 100$), results in a "whole" number that is symbolic of a unity after division, a perfection and all-inclusiveness, with echoes of both the ten spheres (foundations of cosmology) and the Ten Commandments (foundations of Law): if God is one, the monad which generates all numbers and thus forms the "number base of Creation," then the decade is the monad "extended to include all numbers."[25] Ten is, in other words, God *in* His work, a relationship with multiple resonances to Gower's *In Praise of Peace*: e.g., creator to creation, poet to poem, king to state. In this vision of political concord, the divisive multiplicity of society, so elaborately detailed in the *Cronica Tripertita*, is pushed again and again toward a complete and felicitous complicity.

The present division of England, in this structural encoding, is symbolized by the primary run of the poem, with its nine divisions, since nine, lacking the fullness of ten, is an incipient number that came to represent man in his mortal movement toward perfection. The number thereby became associated with prayer, where man turns, in his defection, toward the one God who perfects him, a yearning that strikes at the very core of Gower's moral ethic.[26] But Gower's numerology works at another level, too, as it is from this division

---

[24] Each of the stanzas begins with a flourished initial of some kind, but these do not typically extend above or below the line. The first exception to this generality is, not surprisingly, the first line of the poem, which is marked with a four-line, ornately decorated initial. The other "odd" initials are two lines in height and include flourishes that extend vertically through the left margin of the page. These have been marked in my edited text by indents and boldfaced initials. Macaulay, in his edition of the poem, only noted nine larger initials, failing to notice the beginning of the fourth division at line 169 — presumably due to the fact that this stanza begins at the top of a page, where the larger initial is less noticeable.

[25] Peck, "Number as Cosmic Language," pp. 29 and 62. This essay is an indispensable introduction to the numerological rhetoric that so characterizes the Middle Ages.

[26] See, for example, Rabanus Maurus' commentary on Eccelesiasticus 25 (*PL* 109.948) or Jerome's commentary on Ezechiel 7:24 (*PL* 25.238). Note also how the number nine relates to the novena, a nine-day devotional prayer of hope considered especially useful in efforts to recover failing health — something allegorically appropriate to Gower's hopes for England as Henry takes the throne.

that unity is derived: nine is a "circular" number "because it reproduces itself in multiplication,"[27] and it is this kind of productivity that is most appropriate to the state at peace Gower hopes to attain. Between the nine and ten divisions of the poem we find, as a result, hints of both a structural circularity and a moral comprehension that embodies the argument of the whole of the poem as well as its various bits and pieces — and perhaps even the whole of the manuscript in which it is contained. The resulting process is epitomized in Chaucer's translation of Boethius' famed *Consolation of Philosophy*:

> Whoso that seketh sooth by a deep thought, and coveyteth not to ben disseyvid by no mysweyes, lat hym rollen and trenden withynne hymself the lyght of his ynwarde sight; and let hym gaderyn ayein, enclynynge into a compas, the longe moevynges of his thoughtes; and let hym techyn his corage that he hath enclosid and hid in his tresors al that he compasseth or secheth fro withoute.[28]

Thus Gower's is revealed as a poetic logic with a productive circularity, a movement from general to personal and back to general that underscores its natural human applicability.

If a man who can properly read his circumstances has a good chance at survival, the man who can properly figure — for which proper reading of numbers is prerequisite — stands the best chance of all. *In Praise of Peace* is an example of just this, an exercise in (and model for) good reading. It is a poem rich with symbolisms and relationships that are ultimately, like so much of Gower's work, about building a way of thinking coherently in the face of the thickening chaos of the world, a way of constructing something positive in a Creation where everything, even knowledge, is invariably tainted by the Fall and what Chaucer (again translating from Boethius) calls "the blake cloude of errour."[29] Gower combines this authorized reasoning — authorized by both his old books and his own place as creator and observer — with his epistemology of reading, and the result is a theory of knowledge rooted in the precision and empirical geometries of mathematics, which can root out unquestionable truths and extrapolate firm conclusions.[30] It is this epistemological conclusion, with its attendant call for rational behavior on the part of all men, that Gower builds into the form and substance of *In Praise of Peace*, thereby fashioning a mathematical proof in the guise of poetry.[31] His theorem: the best rule is that which leads to peace.[32]

---

[27] Peck ("Number as Cosmic Language," p. 62), who provides the demonstration of the number's circularity in action: 2x9=18, 1+8=9; 3x9=27, 2+7=9; etc.

[28] Chaucer, *Boece* 3.me.11.1–9.

[29] "And thanne thilke thing that the blake cloude of errour whilom hadde ycovered schal lighte more clerly than Phebus hymself ne schyneth" (Chaucer, *Boece*, 3.me.11.9–12). For a brief account of the ramifications of the entrance of error into the world with the Fall, see Augustine, *Enchiridion* 17. For extended discussion of Gower's understanding of humankind's functioning in the resultant entropic world, especially in its conjunction with the *Confessio*, see Peck, "John Gower: Editor."

[30] Unquestionable and firm to Gower, that is. We ourselves, living in an age following the discovery of non-Euclidean elliptic, hyperbolic, and spheric geometries, improbability theorems, and theories of uncertainty, are not so lucky.

[31] On the fact that Gower's poetry is itself a harmonizing influence in the world, see Yeager, *John Gower's Poetic.*

[32] I have imported a mathematical vocabulary for this discussion of the poem in order to under-

1 (lines 1–105). In the first of the ten sections of this poetic proof, Gower presents his first step, in which he argues that humility is preferable to vanity. He begins by renewing in the vernacular the praise he gave to Henry in the Latin proem. But, just as in the Latin, Gower moves quickly to observations on God's action in lifting Henry to the glory he now enjoys (stanza 1). Still bearing in mind the divine power and right, Gower introduces Henry's claims to the throne before noting that the land is bound to serve the king and to preserve the harmony of creation (stanzas 2–3). Creation logically leads to another reminder of God's active hand in the world, after which Gower presents himself with full (and exemplifying) humility as an advisor to the king, complimenting Henry on being well read — perhaps thus alluding to the *Confessio*, which, as we have already begun to see, is a constantly present background to the ebb and flow of this poem's particulars (stanza 4). The topic of kings provides Gower with a fitting segue into two exempla of kingship: the first of Solomon, who ruled through reason; the second of Alexander, who ruled through the sword. Gower does not here directly refer to the fall of the former (about which I will say more), but he is swift to note the latter's doom, a failure that the poet attributes to a lack of Christ's presence in the king's life (stanzas 5–7). In contrast, Henry lives under Christ and thus must rule with "pité and grace" (line 52). Central to this corollary is Gower's claim that there is a "lawe of riht" that "schal noght be leid aside" (line 56). Unsaid, but very much implied, is the perception that Richard had set the law aside for his own purposes and thus brought disaster down on England. Gower thus points out that the exception to ruling with "pité and grace" is to make war in order to reclaim that very law. The case in point for Gower (and his audience) is Henry's use of arms to reestablish his rights as an English nobleman, "to cleime and axe his rightful heritage" (line 59). Gower extends this exception to discuss the nature of just war (stanza 10), while still maintaining his theoretical framework that peace should be sustained whenever possible (stanza 11). Gower then directly advises the king to "tak pes on honde" (line 83) in accordance with Christ's teachings (stanza 12). This address leads the poet into a magnificent stanza delineating the virtue of peace (stanza 13), after which he again advises the king to eschew war. This time, however, the appeal is not just to Christian teaching, but to Gower's "olde bokes" (line 96), the authority of antiquity (stanza 14). What was a Christian appeal thus becomes a humanist appeal as Gower concludes this initial section of the poem by turning his old books into history and an appeal to experience as he reminds the king that the famed conquerors of the past are all dead (stanza 15). War is nothing more than vanity, which, unlike humility, is no virtue at all. Indeed, it is associated with the growing specter of Pride, the first of vices and subject of Book 1 of the *Confessio*,

---

score the importance of axiomatic logic in Gower's thinking. In this regard it is important for us to remember that Gower lived long before the mathematical revolutions of the nineteenth century in which the long-held assumptions of Euclidean geometry — namely, the five postulates in Euclid's *Elements* from which he derived his 465 propositions of basic geometry — were put into question by the work of Gauss, Bolyai, and Lobachevsky, among others (see also note 29, above). The axiomatic method, for Gower, was uniform and consistent, and Euclid's assumptions were considered self-evident. Some of the key mathematical terms I will be using in this section, for those unfamiliar with them: *theorem* (a proposition to be proved on the basis of explicit assumptions), *lemma* (a statement that could be the final conclusion of an argument but is being used to form part of a proof of a more substantial theorem), *corollary* (a proposition that can be easily deduced from a proposition already given), *claim* (a minor, but necessary or very interesting, proven result that can be used in proving another proposition), and *remark* (a claim presented without proof, usually assumed to be obvious).

whose entry into the poem was prepared in the humility tropes at the very opening of *In Praise of Peace*.

2 (lines 106–47). Gower's lemma that war is nothing more than vanity moves him into the second section of the poem, a six-stanza delineation of the dangers of war, evidence to support his theory that peace is best. He calls war the mother of all wrongs (line 106), a proposition that he supports with evidence: war harms the Church, women, and the cities, and it overthrows the proper rules of Law, which ought to govern all (stanza 16). Indeed, he points out, war harms the whole of "the comon poeple" (line 114) such that even the victors do not truly get security (stanza 17). This remark set forth, Gower determines that the king, since his primary duty is to protect his people, is both physician and redeemer to the land by practicing peace (stanza 18). Gower then tests this second lemma through suppositional logic and historical example by noting that warmongering counselors, if they should arise, must not be listened to: God should be the king's foremost counsel (stanza 19). Here the poet once again recalls Richard without actually naming the deposed king, since Richard was widely regarded as a ruler who listened too often to wicked councillors and thus harmed his country. (This was one of Gower's foremost complaints, for example, in the *Cronica Tripertita*.) Since, as Gower reasserts, the king must always look to the protection of the homeland (stanza 20), he should therefore look to good counsel. And good counsel, Gower concludes, begins with "resonable" thinking, "wittes stable" (lines 144–45) that produce proper understandings such that the king might make his own decisions. Good counsel therefore functions both without and within, guided by wisdom inspired by the greater King, Christ who rules in Heaven (stanza 21).

3 (lines 148–68). The third section of the poem builds up from the foundation that Gower established in the second: the subject of Christ turns the poet to discussion of Scripture and its fulfillment in the Word. Bloodshed is perilous, Gower says, so there is real honor only in peace (stanzas 22–23). He appeals this time not to old books but to "holi bokes" (line 163), and aptly calls the king's attention to the long-standing allegory of Christ as the head of the Church that is humanity. So, too, is the relationship between subjects and their secular sovereigns, a parallel that the king should take to both heart and head (stanza 24).

4 (lines 169–96). One topic leads smoothly to another as Gower's proof advances, the proposition of Christian ethics in the third section recalling in the fourth the examples of first the Ten Commandments and then Christ's own words — all of which advise peace (stanzas 25–26). The corollary recollection of Mosaic Law spurs Gower to note that the Jews lived in peace with one another, though they fought many wars with the pagans who opposed them. The nations of Christendom, since Christianity is a more complete faith than Judaism, are therefore especially wrong in fighting internally (stanza 27). Gower then culminates the first four parts of his poem with the conclusion that the goal of the death of Christ, indeed the whole point of Advent, was "[t]o give ous pes" (line 190). Christendom's inability to unite peacefully thus denies Christ "His dewe reverence" (line 196).

5 (lines 197–252). The poem's fifth section takes as its cue Gower's lemma that Christ died for peace: How well, then, Gower asks, has the Church followed His teachings? The poet begins with the observation that knighthood is meant to defend the Church and thus ought to be the duty of "everi man" under the direction of Christ as Prince of Peace (line 199). But reality falls far short of such an ideal. Most knights serve the state for themselves, not God, and the perilous state of Christendom during the Great Schism means that a king like Henry has a greater role than ever before: he must not only rule England, he must be mindful of the larger role of Christian knight-protector (stanza 29). Gower remarks on the unfortunate desire for fame and worldly desire among most of his contemporary knights, carefully leading to his observation that even the papacy stands amiss in misguidedly calling for wars against the pagan outside when chaos yet reigns within its own house (stanza 30). The actuality of the Church is thus juxtaposed with Christ's intention (stanza 31), an un-favorable comparison that recalls to Gower's mind once more the pressing fact of internal dissent in Christendom (stanza 32). Gower's apparently inevitable, if somewhat shocking and bold, conclusion is that guidance, at least for the moment, is not to be had in the pope. The Church is bigger than the papacy. Its true Head, the poet reminds us, is Christ. So it can be maintained by kings through the sustaining power of law which is "resonable" to "mannys wit" (line 237). Internal guidance thus once again becomes the keystone to proper rule (stanzas 33–34). Lest he be termed a Wycliffite, however (an accusation that would no doubt horrify him), Gower concludes with the optimistic hope that knights will return to the proper task of defending the Church, and that the Church and the states will thereby come together to follow the greater King of Heaven in a unity that will preserve them against outward threats such as the rising Saracens in the East (stanzas 35–36). The point is not that Henry (or any other Christian prince) should embark on crusade; rather, it is that a good king should assist in making and sustaining wise clerical appointments at home so that Christendom might dwell in peace.

   6 (lines 253–94). What stands in the way of proper Christian unity makes up the sixth section of *In Praise of Peace*, five stanzas in which Gower enumerates three points by which Christ's peace stands "oppressed" (line 253). The first of these points, just mentioned in the poem, is the internal divisions within the Church and Christendom (stanza 37). The second point is improper rule since, as Gower allegorizes, if the head is sick the limbs will ache (line 260). In other words, such error leads to war and avarice among Christian lands, conflicts that further disturb Christian peace. The third point is a direct result of the first two, Gower posits: outsiders, seeing the dissension and lack of proper rule within the borders of Chris-tendom, are more likely to attack. And since the Church has failed to keep the Law that limits such improper behavior, hope for overcoming these three faults stands in good secular rule. In particular, for Gower, the hope falls upon the king and his embrace of peace (stanza 39). The poet again reminds the king of the limitations of mortal life which, whatever else one might say about it, is short: the king should think of the postmortem effects of his actions and how only commitment to Christ and His peace will garner lasting rewards (stanza 40). As evi-dence for this proposition, Gower turns to the most famous grouping of worldly powers in the Middle Ages, the Nine Worthies. Rather than listing their accomplishments, Gower here leaves them as bare names, symbols of vanity who are all, despite their great conquests and victories, dead. In light of mortality, he says, peace is best (stanzas 41–42).

   7 (lines 295–329). Gower uses each step of his proof as foundation for the next. This time, his lemma that peace is more a guarantor of salvation than conquest sets the stage for the seventh section of his poem, in which he argues for a deeds-based theology. He begins here with the examples of tennis and wool-spinning to show that a charitable ethic is not a random game of chance (stanza 43). Peace is, rather, a natural, divinely endorsed position that ought to be maintained through the free choice of men (stanza 44). These turns of the-ology — mixing natural law and free will — move Gower to conclude that "pes is, as it were, a sacrement" (line 309). Right worship of God is thereby revealed in submission to a peaceful ethic both in action and in inner belief (stanza 45). Given the disarray of the papacy, the king is thus made to occupy a priestly role for his people and the English Church, as well, standing before God and acting with honest good will ("Withouten eny double entendement," line

311) to conduct the state safely toward peace.[33] Gower argues, then, for a deeds-based theology, one founded largely on charity (stanza 46), and he finds scriptural basis for such a theology in Paul's conclusions that charity precludes war (stanza 47).

8 (lines 330–57). Gower begins the eighth section of his poem by presenting a theoretical basis for his deeds-based theology, observing that such a view is given in the authorized writings of Cassiodorus, who says that pity provides grace and peace through the hand of mercy (stanza 48). Pity and mercy thus become the driving themes to the story of Constantine and Silvester, in which Constantine learns that he might prolong his own life by murdering young children. This he refuses to do. God returns this pity to the emperor by sending Pope Silvester who heals and baptizes him, making "him hol at al" (line 345). And with the conversion of Constantine came the conversion of Rome: "Thus schal pité be preised evermore" (line 357). In the *Confessio* Gower had presented this tale as an example of how "charité mai helpe a man / In bothe worldes" (2.3498–99). Here, it functions not only as a testament to the virtue of pity, but also as a final proof to Gower's long and careful logic in the poem: reason, supported by example, is the finest guide.

9 (lines 358–78). The ninth section of the proof-poem circles back to the opening,[34] as Gower returns to praise of Henry in a final, long, and direct appeal that he rule England with pity — since pity, the poet has already shown, leads to peace (stanzas 52–53).[35] The king, Gower argues, must turn inward to the "conscience" God has "planted" within him (line 368). He might thereby take his place among the saints in fulfilling Christ's will, earning eternal glory. Even more, the poet reminds the king of his earlier proposition that peace can gain a ruler "erthli pris" (line 372). Gower then affirms his own allegiance to Henry, placing himself in the role of the proper counselor who is the complement to a good king — which reminds us of Gower's comments on (and prayers for) the crown at the end of the *Confessio*, as well as the counselor/counseled relationship of the poet's own duality in Genius/Amans.

10 (lines 379–85). But the poet is not finished. The tenth and final section of his proof, comprising a single, envoy-like stanza, shifts the audience of *In Praise of Peace* from Henry to all of Christendom. In these final lines Gower efficiently restates the whole of his proof in its general applicability to all rulers, his verse filled with active and imperative verbs: cease war, restore the papacy, be charitable, hold pity, and maintain law. Only then will peace come to reign over all.

---

[33] Note that earlier, at the beginning of the 1390s, Gower had looked to the clergy "to praie and to procure" peace on earth "[a]ftir the reule of charité" and "[t]his lond amende" (*CA* 8.2995– 3005) — perhaps because the first estate, in Richard, had failed to provide adequate guidance (compare these lines in the first recension). By the end of Richard's reign, however, it was clear that the second estate had also failed to produce peace as the church continued to struggle under partisan behavior from a papacy promoting crusades against other segments of Christendom; the first estate (for England, at least) needed to assume reasonable leadership of the church. In late 1399, with Henry on the throne and seemingly backed by the second estate (see, e.g., the *Cronica Tripertita* on the role of Arundel and others in the restoration of authority in England), there was a new chance for the first estate to govern the whole of the kingdom responsibly, as it should.

[34] On the fitting circularity inherent in the number nine, see note 27, above.

[35] Gower had made Pity the fourth part of Policy in the *Confessio*, citing more exempla for the virtue than he does for any other. As he writes in concluding that discussion: "I mai argue / That Pité is the foundement / Of every kinges regiment, / If it be medled with justice. / Thei tuo remuen alle vice, / And ben of vertu most vailable / To make a kinges regne stable" (*CA* 7.4196–4202).

In Praise of Peace is thus not simply a straightforward polemic against war. It is the result of a subtle craft, one that is wisely attuned to the fundamental problem of giving advice to kings who hold the very unsubtle power of capital punishment. Judith Ferster terms this dangerous business a "dance of deference and delicate challenge,"[36] and Gower can indeed be at pains to perform rhetorical gymnastics as he advises peace to a king who achieved the crown by conquest. But Gower, for all the anxieties that must have attended in this tricky task of telling one's sovereign how to act, apparently could not abandon the role of councillor. If not quite utopian in his outlook, Gower seems ever to have been the wary optimist.[37]

To be sure, Gower would have somewhat of a vested interest in being subtle in such work; as Strohm has pointed out, "most advice-giving to medieval kings" is inevitably full of "generous quantities of flattery, programmatic conciliation, wary evasion, and self-protective equivocation."[38] But there is something deeper than this in Gower's work, something less reticent, that comes across especially when his work is addressed to Henry. Whatever the specifics of their relationship, it seems to have been a close one insofar as it provided to Gower the confidence to speak safely, if not the whole of his mind, at least far more than most of his fellow countrymen would dare.[39] When Gower alters his presentations of Solomon and Alexander from those found in the *Confessio* to those found in *In Praise of Peace*, doing so in order to provide the exemplum of a wise king who does not fall and a belligerent conqueror who does, Grady argues that "Gower cannot paint Henry as a new Alexander in a poem advising the king to establish a rule of peace, but neither can he accurately characterize him as a modern Solomon, because of Henry's route to power (which, if it is not to be ignored, must be legitimized)."[40] While issues of legitimization cannot be denied in a poem which directly confronts them,[41] Gower is surely not hoping for any ignorance on

---

[36] Ferster, *Fictions of Advice*, p. 88. Ferster's work is fundamental to any understanding of the mirror for princes genre and its function in the late Middle Ages. Her chapter on Gower ("O Political Gower," pp. 108–36) is of obvious relevance to the present subject, though the difficulties of giving advice to those holding authority is one that is traced throughout her text.

[37] Or perhaps a "dark" optimist, especially if one accepts some of the more foreboding readings of his work — e.g., Hugh White's reading of the conclusion to the *Confessio* (*Nature, Sex, and Goodness*, pp. 202–19). Still, in most of his work, *In Praise of Peace* included, Gower ultimately seems conditionally positive in outlook even if practically wary in experience. Though he might not *expect* England to become Eden, he *hopes* for it to occur. And although he is aware of the inherent uncertainties of communication, still he writes.

[38] Strohm, *England's Empty Throne*, p. 175.

[39] Grady begins his discussion of *In Praise of Peace* by comparing Henry's response to the advice given him by friend Philip Repyngdon with that given him by William Norham. The former, whose work has a number of similarities of theme with Gower's (Henry as hand of God, an unrestful kingdom, the need for peace within the land), managed to become bishop of Lincoln under Henry. The latter, a hermit who rebuked the king, was beheaded. See "Lancastrian Gower," pp. 552–53.

[40] Grady, "Lancastrian Gower," p. 565. Gower similarly alters his presentation of Constantine in this poem.

[41] Here, too, however, Gower's confidence in addressing the king is borne out. Fisher notes that during Henry's 30 September 1399 address to Parliament, "Henry had proposed that he claim the throne by conquest, but Chief Justice Thirning had objected on the ground that a conqueror is under no obligation to respect the laws, lives, and property of his subjects. . . . [I]t is significant that Gower adopted the Chief Justice's position rather than Henry's own" (*John Gower*, p. 132).

Henry's part concerning these stories. He is not fumbling with his sources in an attempt to make such a rhetorical and political parry. Quite to the contrary, Gower is *relying* on Henry to fill in the relevant blanks for himself. He fully anticipates and expects Henry to be aware of the ill end suffered by Solomon, for example. Henry's present moment is perhaps his zenith, and it is given appropriate parallel in the zenith of Solomon's good fortunes. The ironic juxtaposition, given Gower's glossing over of Solomon's ultimate fate, heightens the unspoken but ever-present threat to Henry's own future. Henry needs only to learn to read it for himself. This would, after all, be the mark of the good student addressed in the *Confessio*.

For all his subtlety, then, Gower is never unclear. He does not equivocate. His positions on the underlying problems that he perceives to be plaguing his society do not change over the course of his career, even as the surface conditions of those problems do. Henry might replace Richard as king, but he faces the same difficulties of kingship. The men beneath the crown are interchangeable, but the crown itself remains as a symbol for something greater than the men who wear it: they do so on what is clearly borrowed time.[42] By the same token, Gower attacks the Church and the papacy for their lack of unity even while pledging his unflagging support for the estate of the Church and the position of the pope as ideals.[43] Indeed, Gower makes the point of borrowed time explicit in the latter half of the poem (lines 281–87), when he calls Henry's attention to the Nine Worthies, military victors all, who here serve not as inspiring models of conquest, but as figures of vainglory who share one characteristic above all else: they have all gone to meet their maker.

The Trentham Manuscript

The text provided here is from the sole surviving copy, that of London, British Library MS Additional 59495, known to Macaulay and earlier editors as the Trentham Manuscipt. This manuscript, composed entirely of Gower's work, is interesting in its own right, and it is worth commenting briefly on its history.[44] According to various notations in the manuscript, it passed from one Charles Gedde to Thomas Fairfax on 28 June 1656.[45] Then, later that same year, Fairfax gave the book to Thomas Gower.[46] Before relinquishing the volume to Thomas Gower, however, Fairfax summarized its contents on the first folio: "Sir John Gower's learned poems: the same booke by himself presented to Kinge Henry the Fourth before his coro-

---

[42] For more on the crown in Gower, see especially *CA* 7.1751–74, where Gower extends his symbolic readings to include the various individual elements of the crown that together signify the primary virtues of proper kingship. A similar discussion occurs in *Richard the Redeless* 1.33–48.

[43] It is this loyalty to the ideal that sets Gower so clearly apart from reformers like the Lollards, who had determined that ecclesiastical positions were by their nature tainted. In colloquial terms, Gower would no doubt accuse the Lollards of throwing the baby out with the bathwater.

[44] Macaulay provides a fine description of the manuscript and its contents (1.lxxix–lxxxiii), which I have confirmed by consultation with facsimiles of the manuscript itself. He includes most of the various notations on the manuscript, along with some discussion.

[45] See, in particular, the notations on fol. 39v, where Gedde writes "This booke pertaineth to aged Charles Gedde," who claims in a preceding notation that he was seventy years old in 1651. To this, Fairfax has added: "but now to Fairfax of his gift, Jun. 28. 1656."

[46] Fol. 1r: "For my honorable freind & kinsman / Sʳ. Thomas Gower knt. and Baronett from / Fairfax 1656."

nation." Fairfax's claim that Trentham is a presentation copy that was given to Henry by Gower himself is difficult to sustain: if nothing else, we would expect a copy of such royal aspirations to be more remarkable in its design and execution. Yet the manuscript's connection to Henry is strong enough to suggest that perhaps Trentham is the master from which such a presentation volume was copied. That is, Gower directed the composition of Trentham, then caused a more elaborate copy to be made and given to the king. The original then passed somehow from Gower's hands to those of Gedde, perhaps making its way through the library of the earl of Richmond, later Henry VII, at some point during its journey.[47]

The claims of royal connection certainly move us toward consideration of the manuscript's audience, itself a topic related to its contents. A manuscript of only forty-one leaves, Trentham's contents can be divided into roughly seven works:

1. Fols. 5r–10v: The English poem *In Praise of Peace* (the unique copy).
2. Fols. 10v–11r: The Latin poem *Rex celi deus*.
3. Fols. 11v–12v: Two French balades that bookend a Latin poem combining *O recolende* and *H. aquile pullus*. Macaulay (1.335–37) refers to this sequence as the "Dedication" to the *Cinkante Balades* and prints it as such (a unique combination).
4. Fols. 12v–33r: The French sequence *Cinkante Balades* (the unique copy).
5. Fol. 33v: The Latin poem *Ecce patet tensus*, which ends imperfectly due to a missing folio (the unique copy).
6. Fols. 34r–39r: The French sequence *Traitié pour ensampler les amantz marietz*, which begins imperfectly due to a missing folio.
7. Fol. 39v: The Latin poem *Quicquid homo scribat* (in a unique version), which appears to have been a later addition to the manuscript.

One of the first things that is striking about this list of contents is the trilingual quality of the Trentham Manuscript. Nowhere, I think, is Gower's fluid and effective movement between English, Latin, and French more clearly and briefly seen than in this unique manuscript.[48] The second point of particular interest is Henry's explicit or implicit presence in the material collected within its leaves. *In Praise of Peace* is directly addressed to Henry, of course, and *Rex celi deus* follows its English precedent in celebrating Henry's arrival and asking the king to follow the example of Christ in ruling his new-won kingdom. The first balade of the mixed French and Latin Dedication to the *Cinkante Balades*, too, follows the pattern of lauding Henry, beginning with the claim that Henry is a king due to divine intervention,

---

[47] On fol. 2v the name of "Rychemond" is recorded, along with a sixteenth-century inscription: "Liber Hen: Septimi tunc comitis Richmond / manu propria script." The other primary clue to its provenance is the cut-off words "Will Sanders vn Just . . ." on fol. 41r, the last leaf of the manuscript. Macaulay comments on its life between Gower and Gedde: "if we are to regard the signature 'Rychemond' on the second leaf as a genuine autograph of Henry VII while Earl of Richmond, it would seem that the book passed at some time into royal hands, but it can hardly have come to the Earl of Richmond by any succession from Henry IV" (1.lxxxii).

[48] Echard observes that our awareness of Gower's linguistic variability is somewhat hindered by Macaulay's printing of Gower's works by their languages, which results in a view of Gower that does not accord well with what we find in Trentham, for example, a manuscript that "may well have been put together around 1400 specifically to showcase Gower's skills while honouring Henry IV's coronation. That is, the Trentham MS has particular and linguistic themes which become muted in Macaulay's rearrangement of its contents" ("Gower in Print," p. 133).

then focusing on both Henry's wondrous characteristics ("pity, prowess, humility, royal honor," he writes in line 1) and on Gower's place as "humble vassal" (line 15) and subject. The Latin poem that follows the first balade comprises the first eight lines of *O recolende*,[49] attached to the four-line poem *H. aquile pullus* — both of which likewise follow the themes laid out in the initial English poem, taking as their subject both the praising of the king and the counsel that he should engage in a moral, peaceful rule. At the end of this conflated Latin poem there are two quotations from the Vulgate that function as blessings on the new-crowned king: Vulgate Psalms 88:23 ("The enemy shall have no advantage over him: nor the son of iniquity have power to hurt him") and 40:2 ("The Lord preserve him and give him life, and make him blessed upon the earth: and deliver him not up to the will of his enemies"). The second French balade of the Dedication is imperfect (fol. 12 being considerably damaged), but what we can read indicates that the balades which follow the Dedication were composed for presentation at Henry's court.[50] And while the *Cinkante Balades*, a collected sequence not unlike Petrarch's sonnets, do not make explicit reference to the people of the royal court, it is not difficult to see the sequence as just what it claims to be: royal entertainment rather than personal autobiography. The envoy of the *Cinkante Balades* would also appear to confirm such a scenario, addressing the work to both England and its noble king, Henry. Following this long French sequence, the short Latin poem *Ecce patet tensus* continues the themes of Love's power that were so subtly expressed in the preceding balades, while also providing a segue into the French *Traitié*, another series of balades, this time eighteen in number, with corresponding Latin marginalia that appear, like those of the *Confessio Amantis*, to be both authorial and integral to the poem. The subject of these balades is, like those of the *Cinkante Balades*, love, but it is of a more mature form than the youthful love of the earlier, longer sequence: Gower proposes to advise married lovers on the maintenance of their vows. The manuscript ends with the short Latin poem *Quicquid homo scribat*, in which Gower claims that he lost his sight in the first year of Henry's reign and then, in its final lines, makes one final request of the world (line 12): "That God make our kingdoms prosperous in the future. Amen." This request, which reminds us at once of Gower's final prayer for England at the end of the *Confessio*, brings the poet and the manuscript full circle: what began in hope, with praise of Henry and humble requests for a rule of peace to bring England out from the ashes of Richard's reign and restore it to proper rule, has passed through times of sheer joy only to end with a return to prayer on behalf of his nation. Seen in such light, one might view Gower as considering Henry's coronation a marker of his own return from exile, in which the voice in the wilderness is finally brought into the fold of the royal court to entertain his prince. If so, then the Trentham Manuscript reveals not only the initial optimism of this progression but also the scarcely veiled pessimism of its ultimate result: a return to a kind of exile as Gower retires to St. Mary Overeys claiming blindness and infirmity, turning over his pen to poets whose youth would allow them the kind of idealistic optimism that time and experience had taken from him. Indeed, his subsequent poems, from *Presul ouile regis* to *Orate pro anima*, make clear that Henry's coming had not cleansed his country of its ills. The death of Richard was not that of the

---

[49] Macaulay observes that the ninth line ought probably to have been written in as well, since the grammar does not make much sense in its extant form (1.461).

[50] Macaulay notes that this would stand against Warton, the critic who first brought attention to the sequence and considered it to be from Gower's youth, perhaps ca. 1350 (1.lxxi–lxxii).

phoenix. The poet's hopes had not been fulfilled. Gower could still see the metaphorical blemishes of plague spotting the land, and his poetry thereby turns, slowly and inexorably, to the final theme of death.

NOTE ON THE TEXT

The poem's divisions, marked by larger, two-line initials, are here shown by indentation and boldface initials. An early printed text was produced in Thynne's edition of *Chaucer's Works* (though not attributed to Chaucer), and Thynne's readings are given where this present text diverges significantly from Macaulay's. For a full apparatus comparing the text with that of Thynne, see Macaulay's edition (3.481–92).

Electus Cristi, pie Rex Henrice, fuisti,
Qui bene venisti cum propria regna petisti,
Tu mala vicisti que bonis bona restituisti,
Et populo tristi nova gaudia contribuisti.
Est michi spes lata quod adhuc per te renovata
Succedent fata veteri probitate beata,
Est tibi nam grata gracia sponte data.

[Dutiful King Henry, who was chosen by Christ,
Who rightfully came and sought a special reign,
You conquered evil and by good restored the good,
And to the sorrowful people you gave new joys.
I have hope for what you have brought because thus far what you have restored
Will raise up through honest blessing what was said of old,
You have hence given a pleasing grace by your own free will.]

1.

    O worthi noble kyng, Henry the Ferthe,   *Fourth*
In whom the glade fortune is befalle   *On; good fortune has befallen*
The poeple to governe uppon this erthe,
God hath thee chose in comfort of ous alle: *chosen to comfort us*
5   The worschipe of this lond, which was doun falle,   *honor; had fallen down*
Now stant upriht thurgh grace of thi goodnesse,   *stands raised*
Which every man is holde for to blesse.   *meant to bless*

2.

The highe God of His justice allone   *judgment alone*
The right which longeth to thi regalie   *attends; royalty*
10   Declared hath to stonde in thi persone.   *Has declared to belong*
And more than God may no man justefie.
Thi title is knowe uppon thin ancestrie,   *founded upon your*
The londes folk hath ek thy riht affermed;   *people of the land have also*
So stant thi regne of God and man confermed.   *stands your reign*

3.

15   Ther is no man mai seie in other wise,   *say to the contrary*
That God Himself ne hath thi riht declared;   *has not your right*

Wherof the lond is boun to thi servise,   *Therefore; bound*
Which for defalte of help hath longe cared.   *lack of aid has long suffered*
Bot now ther is no mannes herte spared   *man's heart*
20   To love and serve and wirche thi plesance: *work your pleasure*
And al is this thurgh Godes pourveiance.   *God's working*

4.
In alle thing which is of God begonne   *(i.e., all Creation)*
Ther folwith grace, if it be wel governed: *follows*
Thus tellen thei whiche olde bookes conne,   *know*
25   Whereof, my lord, Y wot wel thow art lerned.   *I know well [that] you are learned*
Axe of thi God, so schalt thou noght be werned   *Ask; refused*
Of no reqweste whiche is resonable;
For God unto the goode is favorable.   *the good*

5.
Kyng Salomon, which hadde at his axinge   *Solomon; asking*
30   Of God what thing him was levest to crave,   *he most desired to have*
He ches wisdom unto the governynge   *chose*
Of Goddis folk, the whiche he wolde save: *people, whom he would*
And as he ches, it fel him for to have;   *chose, [so] it came down to him to have*
For thurgh his wit, whil that his regne laste,   *reign lasted*
35   He gat him pees and reste into the laste.   *won peace; until the end*

6.
Bot Alisaundre, as telleth his histoire,   *Alexander [the Great]*
Unto the God besoghte in other weie: *another way*
Of all the world to winne the victoire,
So that undir his swerd it myht obeie.   *might obey [him]*
40   In werre he hadde al that he wolde preie —   *war; desire*
The myghti God behight him that beheste —   *granted*
The world he wan, and had it of conqweste.   *[So]; won*

7.
Bot thogh it fel at thilke time so,   *though it happened at that time*
That Alisandre his axinge hath achieved,
45   This sinful world was al paiene tho,   *pagan then*
Was non which hath the hihe God believed;   *[There] was none who; high (i.e., true)*
No wondir was thogh thilke world was grieved.   *It was no wonder then that the*
Thogh a tiraunt his pourpos myhte winne: *Then*
Al was vengance and infortune of sinne.

8.
50   Bot now the feith of Crist is come a place   *has come [to have] a place*
Among the princes in this erthe hiere,   *on; here*
It sit hem wel to do pité and grace.   *well befits them (i.e., the princes); pity*
Bot yit it mot be tempred in manere: *Nonetheless it might be tempered in due measure*

For as thei finden cause in the matiere   *matter*
55   Uppon the point, what aftirward betide,   *At hand, whatever [may] afterward occur*
The lawe of riht schal noght be leid aside.   *laid aside*

9.

So mai a kyng of werre the viage   *war the journey*
Ordeigne and take, as he therto is holde,   *he is made to do*
To cleime and axe his rightful heritage   *claim and demand*
60   In alle places wher it is withholde.   *withheld*
Bot otherwise, if God Himsilve wolde   *But in other cases*
Afferme love and pes betwen the kynges,   *peace*
Pes is the beste above alle erthely thinges.

10.

Good is t'eschue werre, and natheles   *to eschew war, and nonetheless*
65   A kyng may make werre uppon his right,
For of bataile the final ende is pees.   *battle; peace*
Thus stant the lawe, that a worthi knyght   *stands*
Uppon his trouthe may go to the fight.
Bot if so were that he myghte chese,   *But if it happened; choose*
70   Betre is the pees, of which may no man lese.   *lose*

11.

Sustene pes oghte every man alyve,   *To sustain peace ought*
First for to sette his liege lord in reste,   *in rest (at ease)*
And ek these othre men that thei ne stryve;   *also; they might not fight*
For so this world mai stonden ate beste.   *thus*
75   What kyng that wolde be the worthieste,   *would be the most worthy*
The more he myghte oure dedly werre cesse,   *deadly war cease*
The more he schulde his worthinesse encresse.   *increase*

12.

Pes is the chief of al the worldes welthe,   *world's riches*
And to the Heven it ledeth ek the weie.   *Heaven it also leads the way*
80   Pes is of soule and lif the mannes helthe: *a man's health in soul and body*
Of pestilence and doth the werre aweie!   *[Be rid]; send the war away*
Mi liege lord, tak hiede of that Y seie: *take heed of what I say*
If werre may be left, tak pes on honde,   *abandoned; in hand*
Which may noght be withoute Goddis sonde.   *God's message*

13.

85   With pes stant every creature in reste;   *stands*
Withoute pes ther may no lif be glad: *no life can be happy*
Above alle othre good pes is the beste.   *other goods*
Pes hath himself, whan werre is al bestad;   *itself, whereas war is ever afflicted*
The pes is sauf, the werre is ever adrad.   *safe; dreaded*

90 Pes is of al charité the keie,   *key*
    Which hath the lif and soule for to weie.   *weigh*

14.

    My liege lord, if that thee list to seche   *if you want to seek*
    The sothe essamples that the werre hath wroght,   *true examples*
    Thow schalt wiel hiere of wisemennes speche   *You shall well hear*
95 That dedly werre turneth into noght.   *deadly war results in nothing*
    For if these olde bokes be wel soght,   *clearly examined*
    Ther myght thou se what thing the werre hath do,   *has done*
    Bothe of conqueste and conquerour also.

15.

    For vein honour or for the worldes good,   *vain; world's goods*
100 Thei that whilom the stronge werres made,   *great wars*
    Wher be thei now? Bethenk wel in thi mod.   *Think well on this in your mind*
    The day is goon, the nyght is derk and fade,   *gone; dark and faded*
    Her crualté, which mad hem thanne glade,   *Their cruelty, which made them then*
    Thei sorwen now, and yit have noght the more;   *regret; no more chances*
105 The blod is schad, which no man mai restore.   *blood is shed*

16.

    The werre is modir of the wronges alle;
    It sleth the prest in Holi Chirche at Masse,   *slays*
    Forlith the maide and doth here flour to falle.   *Violates; causes her flower to fall*
    The werre makth the grete citee lasse,   *city less*
110 And doth the Lawe his reules overpasse.   *causes the overthrow of the rules of Law*
    There is no thing wherof meschef mai growe
    Which is noght caused of the werre, Y trowe.   *I believe*

17.

    The werre bringth in poverté at hise hieles,   *its heels*
    Wherof the comon poeple is sore grieved;   *Through which the common people are*
115 The werre hath set his cart on thilke whieles   *those wheels*
    Wher that Fortune mai noght be believed.
    For whan men wene best to have achieved,   *think*
    Ful ofte it is al newe to beginne:
    The werre hath no thing siker, thogh he winne.   *sure; even if he wins*

18.

120 Forthi, my worthi prince, in Cristes halve,   *Therefore; on Christ's behalf*
    As for a part whos feith thou hast to guide,   *country*
    Leie to this olde sor a newe salve,   *Apply; old wound*
    And do the werre awei, what so betide.   *whatsoever happens (i.e., regardless of the cost)*
    Pourchace pes, and set it be thi side,   *Purchase peace; by your side*
125 And suffre noght thi poeple be devoured.   *do not allow your people [to] be*
    So schal thi name ever after stonde honoured.

19.

If eny man be now or ever was
Agein the pes thi prevé counseillour,   *private*
Lete God ben of thi counseil in this cas,   *Let God be your counsel*
130 And putte awei the cruel werreiour.   *warrior*
For God, which is of man the creatour,
He wolde noght men slowe His creature   *would not [have] men slay*
Withoute cause of dedly forfeture.   *[a just] cause of mortal danger*

20.

Wher nedeth most, behoveth most to loke.   *need is greatest, that needs most attention*
135 Mi lord, howso thi werres ben withoute,   *regardless of how your foreign wars have gone*
Of time passed who that hiede toke,   *From; heed*
Good were at hom to se riht wel aboute;   *[It] would be good; [the] right thing done for all*
Foreveremor the werste is for to doute.   *worst is to doubt*
Bot if thou myghtest parfit pes atteigne,   *you desire to attain perfect peace*
140 Ther schulde be no cause for to pleigne.   *for [the land] to complain*

21.

Aboute a kyng good counseil is to preise   *praise*
Above alle othre thinges most vailable;   *serviceable*
Bot yit a kyng withinne himself schal peise,   *appraise*
And se the thinges that ben resonable,   *are reasonable*
145 And theruppon he schal his wittes stable   *establish (found)*
Among the men to sette pes in evene,   *equally*
For love of Him which is the Kyng of Hevene.   *(i.e., Christ)*

22.

Ha, wel is him that schedde nevere blod,   *Ah, well*
Bot if it were in cause of rihtwisnesse: *Unless; righteousness*
150 For if a kyng the peril undirstod,
What is to sle the poeple, thanne Y gesse,   *slay the people, then I suppose*
The dedly werres and the hevynesse,
Wherof the pes distourbid is ful ofte,   *very often*
Schulde at som time cesse and wexe softe.   *grow soft*

23.

155 O kyng fulfild of grace and of knyghthode,
Remembre uppon this point for Cristes sake,
If pes be profred unto thi manhode,
Thin honour sauf, let it noght be forsake.   *Your honor [will be] safe*
Though thou the werres darst wel undirtake,   *wars did*
160 Aftir reson yit tempre thi corage.   *temper your courage*
For lich to pes ther is non avantage.   *For compared; no advantage [to war]*

24.

My worthi lord, thenke wel, how so befalle,   *think well*
Of thilke lore. As holi bokes sein,   *Upon such lore*
Crist is the heved, and we ben membres alle,   *head and we are all limbs*
165   Als wel the subgit as the sovereign.   *As well the subjects*
So sit it wel that charité be plein,   *it sits well; plain*
Which unto God Himselve most acordeth,
So as the lore of Cristes word recordeth.

25.

       In th'Olde Lawe, er Crist Himself was bore,   *(i.e., Old Testament), before; born*
170   Among the Ten Comandementz Y rede   *read*
How that manslaghtre schulde be forbore.   *murder; forbidden*
Such was the will that time of the Godhede.   *Godhead (Trinity)*
And aftirward, whanne Crist tok His manhede,   *manhood*
Pes was the ferste thing He let do crie
175   Agein the worldes rancour and envie.

26.

And er Crist wente out of this erthe hiere   *before*
And stigh to Hevene, He made His testament,   *ascended*
Wher He beqwath to His disciples there   *bequeathed*
And gaf His pes, which is the foundement   *foundation*
180   Of charité, withouten whos assent
The worldes pes mai never wel be tried,
Ne love kept, ne lawe justefied.   *Nor*

27.

The Jewes with the paiens hadden werre,   *pagans had war*
Bot thei among hemself stode evere in pes.   *themselves*
185   Whi schulde thanne oure pes stonde out of herre,   *out of order*
Which Crist hath chose unto His oghne encres?   *own increase*
For Crist is more than was Moises,   *Moses*
And Crist hath set the parfit of the Lawe,   *perfection*
The which scholde in no wise be withdrawe.   *no way be withdrawn*

28.

190   To give ous pes was cause whi Crist dide;   *died*
Withoute pes may no thing stonde availed:
Bot now a man mai sen on everi side   *see*
How Cristes feith is every dai assailed,
With the paiens destruid, and so bataurd   *pagans destroyed*
195   That for defalte of help and of defence
Unethe hath Crist His dewe reverence.   *Hardly; due*

29.

    The righte feith to kepe of Holy Chirche
The firste point is named of knyghthode;
And everi man is holde for to wirche   *meant to work*
200   Uppon the point which stant to his manhode.
Bot now, helas, the fame is sprad so broode,   *alas; spread so broad*
That everi worthi man this thing compleigneth,   *complains [about] this thing (fame)*
And yit ther is no man which help ordeigneth.   *ordains*

30.

The worldes cause is waited overal,   *heeded*
205   Ther ben the werres redi to the fulle;
Bot Cristes oghne cause in special,
Ther ben the swerdes and the speres dulle;   *There are the swords; spears*
And with the sentence of the Popes bulle,   *Pope's bull*
As for to do the folk paien obeie,   *to make the pagan folk*
210   The Chirche is turned al another weie.

31.

It is to wondre above a mannys wit   *man's wisdom*
Withoute werre how Cristes feith was wonne;   *victorious*
And we that ben uppon this erthe yit   *yet*
Ne kepe it noght, as it was first begonne.   *begun*
215   To every creature undir the sonne   *sun*
Crist bad Himself how that we schulden preche,
And to the folk His evangile teche.

32.

More light it is to kepe than to make;   *easy; keep; make [something]*
Bot that we founden mad tofore the hond   *what we found made already in [our] hand*
220   We kepe noght, bot lete it lightly slake.   *lessen*
The pes of Crist hath altobroke His bond,   *has broken His bonds asunder*
We reste ourselve and soeffrin every lond   *allow*
To slen ech other as thing undefendid: *slay each other*
So stant the werre, and pes is noght amendid.   *So it is with war*

33.

225   Bot thogh the Heved of Holy Chirche above   *Head (i.e., Christ)*
Ne do noght al His hole businesse
Among the men to sette pes and love,
These kynges oughten of here rightwisnesse   *their righteousness*
Here oghne cause among hemself redresce.   *Their own causes; themselves*
230   Thogh Petres schip as now hath lost his stiere,   *Peter's ship (i.e., the Church); its rudder*
It lith in hem that barge for to stiere.   *fall to them; to steer*

34.

If Holy Cherche after the dueté   *duty*
Of Cristes word ne be noght al avysed   *advised*
To make pes, acord, and unité
235 Among the kinges that ben now devised,   *divided*
Yit natheles the lawe stant assised
Of mannys wit to be so resonable,
Withoute that to stonde hemselve stable.[1]

35.

Of Holy Chirche we ben children alle,
240 And every child is holden for to bowe   *intended to bow*
Unto the modir, how that ever it falle,   *mother*
Or elles he mot reson desalowe: *else he might disallow reason*
And for that cause a knyght schal ferst avowe   *shall first swear*
The right of Holi Chirche to defende,   *The rights*
245 That no man schal the previlege offende.

36.

Thus were it good to setten al in evene
The worldes princes and the prelatz bothe,   *prelates*
For love of Him which is the King of Hevene: *(i.e., Christ)*
And if men scholde algate wexe wrothe,   *should in any case grow angry*
250 The Sarazins, whiche unto Crist be lothe,   *Saracens (i.e., Muslims); are hateful*
Let men ben armed agein hem to fighte;   *against them*
So mai the knyht his dede of armes righte.   *deed*

37.

Uppon thre pointz stant Cristes pes oppressed: *three points Christ's peace stands*
Ferst, Holy Cherche is in hersilf divided,
255 Which oughte of reson first to be redresced;   *redressed*
Bot yit so highe a cause is noght decided.   *high (worthy, noble)*
And thus, whan humble pacience is prided,   *patience*
The remenant, which that thei schulden reule,   *remnant; rule*
No wondir is though it stonde out of reule.   *order*

38.

260 Of that the heved is siek, the limes aken: *When the head is sick, the limbs ache*
These regnes that to Cristes pes belongen   *kings*
For worldes good these dedly werres maken,   *worldly good*
Whiche helpples as in balance hongen.   *helpless; hang*
The heved above hem hath noght undirfongen   *head (Church); undertaken*

---

[1] Lines 236–38: *Yet nevertheless the law has been so well established / By man's wit to be reasonable / That even without that (i.e., the help of the Church) they (the kings) can remain stable*

265	To sette pes, bot every man sleth other;	*slays another*
	And in this wise hath charité no brother.	*way*

39.

	The two defaltes bringen in the thridde,	*faults; third*
	Of mescreantz that sen how we debate;	*miscreants who see*
	Betwene the two thei fallen in amidde,	*the middle*
270	Wher now aldai thei finde an open gate.	*all day (i.e., always)*
	Lo, thus the dedly werre stant algate;	*war stands assuredly*
	Bot evere Y hope of Kyng Henries grace	
	That he it is which schal the pes embrace.	

40.

	My worthi noble prince and kyng enoignt,	*anointed*
275	Whom God hath of His grace so preserved,	
	Beholde and se the world uppon this point,	
	As for thi part that Cristes pes be served:	*your land*
	So schal thin highe mede be deserved	*shall your high reward*
	To him which al schal qwiten ate laste,	*leave at last*
280	For this lif hiere mai no while laste.	

41.

	See Alisandre, Ector, and Julius,	*Alexander, Hector [of Troy], and Julius [Caesar]*
	See Machabeu, David, and Josue,	*[Judas] Maccabeus, [King] David; Joshua*
	See Charlemeine, Godefroi, Arthus,	*Charlemagne, Godfrey [of Bouillon], [King] Arthur*
	Fulfild of werre and of mortalité.	*[Who were] filled with war; death*
285	Here fame abit, bot al is vanité;	*Their fame abides*
	For deth, which hath the werres under fote,	
	Hath mad an ende of which ther is no bote.	*for which there is no remedy*

42.

	So mai a man the sothe wite and knowe,	*truth comprehend*
	That pes is good for every king to have:	
290	The fortune of the werre is evere unknowe,	
	Bot wher pes is, ther ben the marches save.	*there are the borders saved*
	That now is up, tomorwe is under grave;	
	The mighti God hath alle grace in honde,	
	Withouten Him pes mai nought longe stonde.	

43.

295	**Of** the tenetz to winne or lese a chace,	*In the [game of] tennis; lose a chase*
	Mai no lif wite er that the bal be ronne:	*no man know before the ball is run*
	Al stant in God, what thing men schal pourchace,	*All is in God's control; get*
	Th'ende is in Him er that it be begonne.	*The end*
	Men sein the wolle, whanne it is wel sponne,	*strain the wool; spun*
300	Doth that the cloth is strong and profitable,	*So that*
	And elles it mai never be durable.	*otherwise*

44.

The worldes chaunces uppon aventure
Ben evere sett, bot thilke chaunce of pes
Is so behoveli to the creature,   *natural*
305   That it above alle othre is piereles: *peerless*
Bot it mai noght be gete natheles   *expected nevertheless*
Among the men to lasten eny while,   *any long amount of time*
Bot wher the herte is plein withoute guyle.   *Unless; open without guile*

45.

The pes is, as it were, a sacrement
310   Tofore the God, and schal with wordes pleine   *simple*
Withouten eny double entendement   *duplicitous intentions*
Be treted, for the trouthe can noght feine: *entreated; dissemble*
Bot if the men withinne hemself be veine,   *vain*
The substance of the pes may noght be trewe,   *true*
315   Bot every dai it chaungeth uppon newe.   *into [something] new*

46.

Bot who that is of charité parfit,   *perfect*
He voideth alle sleightes ferr aweie,   *slights*
And sett his word uppon the same plit,   *plight*
Wher that his herte hath founde a siker weie: *sure way*
320   And thus whan conscience is trewly weie,
And that the pes be handlid with the wise,   *wisdom*
It schal abide and stonde in alle wise.   *all ways*

47.

Th'apostle seith, ther mai no lif be good   *The apostle (Paul)*
Which is noght grounded uppon charité,
325   For charité ne schedde nevere blod.
So hath the werre as ther no proprité: *property*
For thilke vertu which is seid pité   *that virtue which is called pity*
With charité so ferforth is aqweinted,
That in here may no fals semblant be peinted.   *her may no false seeming*

48.

330   Cassodre, whos writinge is auctorized,   *Cassiodorus; authorized [by the Church]*
Seith, wher that pité regneth, ther is grace,   *Says; reigns*
Thurgh which the pes hath al his welthe assised,   *arranged*
So that of werre he dredeth no manace.   *fears no menace*
Wher pité dwelleth, in the same place
335   Ther mai no dedly cruelté sojorne,   *remain*
Wherof that merci schulde his weie torne.   *way turn*

49.

To se what pité forth with mercy doth,
The croniqe is at Rome in thilke empire   *story; that*
Of Constantin, which is a tale soth;   *Constantine [the Great]; true*
340   Whan him was levere his oghne deth desire   *he would rather die himself*
Than do the yonge children to martire.   *young; murder*
Of crualté he lafte the querele;   *quarrel*
Pité he wroghte and pité was his hele.   *healing*

50.

For thilke mannes pité which he dede   *that; did*
345   God was pitous and mad him hol at al;   *whole*
Silvestre cam, and in the same stede   *[Pope] Silvester; place*
Gaf him baptisme first in special,   *Gave*
Which dide awai the sinne original,   *washed away*
And al his lepre it hath so purified   *leprosy*
350   That his pité forever is magnified.

51.

Pité was cause whi this emperour
Was hol in bodi and in soule bothe,   *whole*
And Rome also was set in thilke honour   *that honor*
Of Cristes feith, so that the lieve of lothe,   *the believers who were once hateful*
355   Whiche hadden be with Crist tofore wrothe,   *Who had been angry at Christ before*
Resceived were unto Cristes lore:
Thus schal pité be preised evermore.   *praised*

52.

My worthi liege lord, Henri be name,   *by name*
Which Engelond hast to governe and righte,   *[hold] upright*
360   Men oghten wel thi pité to proclame,   *ought*
Which openliche in al the worldes sighte   *openly*
Is schewed with the help of God Almighte,
To give ous pes, which longe hath be debated,
Wherof thi pris schal nevere ben abated.   *reward*

53.

365   My lord, in whom hath ever yit be founde
Pité withoute spot of violence,
Kep thilke pes alwei withinne bounde,   *that peace*
Which God hath planted in thi conscience:
So schal the cronique of thi pacience   *history*
370   Among the seintz be take into memoire   *saints be taken into memory*
To the loenge of perdurable gloire.   *praise of eternal glory*

54.

And to thin erthli pris, so as Y can,   *your earthly reward*
Which everi man is holde to commende,
I, Gower, which am al thi liege man,
375   This lettre unto thin excellence Y sende,
As Y which evere unto my lives ende
Wol praie for the stat of thi persone
In worschipe of thi sceptre and of thi throne.

55.

        Noght only to my king of pes Y write,
380   Bot to these othre princes Cristene alle,
That ech of hem his oghne herte endite,   *them his own heart examine*
And see the werre er more meschief falle: *look [to] the war before*
Sette ek the rightful pope uppon his stalle,   *Set also*
Kep charité and draughe pité to honde,
385   Maintene lawe, and so the pes schal stonde.

Explicit carmen de pacis commendacione, quod ad laudem et memoriam serenissimi principis domini Regis Henrici quarti suus humilis orator Iohannes Gower composuit. Et nunc sequitur epistola in qua idem Ioannes pro statu et salute dicti domini sui apud altissimum devocius exorat.

[Here ends the poem on the praising of peace, which John Gower, the humble envoy to King Henry the Fourth, composed for the praise and the remembrance of that most serene prince of the Lord. And now follows the letter in which the same John pleads through the highest devotion for the state and the health of his aforesaid lord.]

[The "epistle" that follows is the Latin poem *Rex celi deus*; see above, pp. 40–43 for that work.]

❧ EXPLANATORY NOTES

ABBREVIATIONS: See p. 55, above.

2   *glade fortune is befalle*. Gower carefully presents a passive verb to open up his initial stanzas on Henry's still-fresh attainment of the crown. The obvious implication is that Henry did not choose the throne for himself. Quite to the contrary, it fell to him through a turn of *glade fortune* for England. Gower's initial defense of Henry is thus set up in Boethian terms: the final years of Richard's reign were both a literal and metaphorical downturn of the realm ("this lond, which was doun falle" — line 5), when ill fortune caused so much ruin. Henry, then, is placed in the role of one who will "raise up" England as he himself is raised up upon the ever-turning wheel of Fortune, a role already alluded to in the sixth of the Latin verses that precede the poem (*Succedent*). That the wheel will not stop turning at the height of Henry's good fortune is not given explicit voice, but the possibility nevertheless looms over the remainder of the poem. Things are good for you now, Gower seems to say, but you must rule well in order to keep a longer grip on the heights of joy. As he says in *O deus immense*, line 68: "Fortune is stable at least in not remaining the same."

4   *God hath thee chose*. Gower reiterates in these opening lines that Henry is not himself responsible for having attained the crown. He is not a conqueror by right of martial arms but a passive tool in the active hand of God. Indeed, God's agency is named directly fourteen times in the first fifty lines of the poem, a remarkable tour de force of divine attribution to what many of his critics considered Henry's all-too-human action.

5   *worschipe*. In addition to the religious import of the term, *worschipe* also functions within a chivalric context, a dual connotation that is particularly fitting for Henry, whose role as a paragon of English chivalry was well known to both his supporters and detractors alike. The poet who wrote *Mum and the Sothsegger*, for example, was happy to portray the new king as a "comely knight ycome of the grettist," a "doughtful doer in deedes of armes," and "the graciousist guyer goyng uppon erthe" (lines 211–20). For more on Henry's martial abilities, see Tuck, "Henry IV and Chivalry."

6   *grace of thi goodnesse*. In crafting a defense of Henry's actions, Gower subtly shifts the king away from being a mere man. Rather, the king belongs to a separate realm of authority, judgment, and respect, a characterization marked by his personal graciousness, but also by the greater grace that is the purveyance of God, that potency beyond mere fortune. See also the note to lines 26–27, below.

12   *uppon thin ancestrie.* The call to ancestry as right of inheritance was often cited
         among supporters of the Lancastrian claim to the crown. The recollection of
         family would have particular weight for Henry himself, who had seen his own
         family lands and rights taken away by Richard. Gower notes in line 13 that the
         people of England have that "riht affermed." See note to line 14.

14   *thi regne of God and man confermed.* Gower carefully builds up a threefold Lancas-
         trian claim to the throne. The first stanza introduced the notion of divine
         election and blessing, that Henry was the chosen instrument of God in taking
         the crown from the ineffectual and unworthy Richard. The second stanza builds
         upon this, adding to it first the notion of Henry's royal descent from Henry III,
         and second the fact that he had been chosen by the people. This latter notion,
         developed as a core trope of the third stanza, probably relates to the assembly's
         election of Henry on 30 September 1399 (see Fisher, *John Gower*, p. 132). Also
         of note for Gower, however, would be the wider aspect of the people, the
         "common" populace who, weary from the rule of Richard, turn to Henry with
         fresh hope for the future. While appropriate to Gower's unfolding purpose,
         these three rationales of blessing, lineage, and election are not the standard
         Lancastrian claims of justification for the usurpation. Quite prominently missing
         is the undeniable fact of Henry's conquest of England. Compare, for example,
         the threefold right to the throne cited by Chaucer in his "Complaint of Chaucer
         to His Purse": "O conquerour of Brutes Albyon, / Which that by lyne and free
         eleccion / Been verray kyng" (lines 23–24). Chaucer is clearly less reticent to
         highlight an admirable martial quality of Henry's prowess.

17–18   *the lond . . . Which for defalte of help hath longe cared.* Gower transfers his percep-
         tion of the suffering of the people of England onto the land, claiming that
         England itself suffered under Richard II. Henry's usurpation will heal the realm
         in body (land) and soul (people).

23   *if it be wel governed.* A none-too-subtle plea on Gower's part, informing Henry
         that God will provide grace under the condition that the king follow his advice.

24–25   *thei whiche olde bookes conne, / Whereof, my lord, Y wot wel thow art lerned.* Grady
         observes that this "forcefully recalls the bookish *Confessio Amantis*, dedicated
         (sometimes) to the bookish Henry Bolingbroke" ("Lancastrian Gower," p. 560).
         The implied connection between the two known English works is no small thing.
         Yeager posits the possibility that "Gower judged Henry a more pragmatic and
         conventionally moral ruler than Richard, one as susceptible to didactic argu-
         ment as . . . he believed Richard was to fictions" (*John Gower's Poetic*, p. 268). If
         so, there is a clear association between the two works dedicated to the king, both
         of which present themselves as written for a primary audience of one: the king
         who must rule rightly in his role as sovereign (compare, in particular, *CA* 7,
         8.2109–20, and 8.3080–3105). Gower, it would seem, expects Henry to have the
         good-rule ethics of the *Confessio* upon his mind as he reads (or hears) *In Praise
         of Peace*. This fact becomes pertinent as Gower begins to recall and then alter
         exempla cited in his earlier English poem. See Peck, "Politics and Psychology,"
         especially pp. 235–37.

26–27   *Axe of thi God . . . resonable.* Just as he did earlier in the poem (see note to line 6), Gower places Henry in the realm of grace. Here, he claims that God will do the will of Henry, a statement that parallels Martha's witness to Christ in John 11:22: "But now also I know that whatsoever thou wilt ask of God, God will give it thee." What saves Gower from heresy is his placing a limit upon the parallel. Henry will, like Christ, get from God what he asks for, providing he is *resonable* (line 27). Gower's trust is primarily in the order of God's universe.

29–35   *Kyng Salomon . . . gat him pees and reste into the laste.* Solomon also plays a prominent role in Book 7 of *CA*, where his wisdom (7.3891–3942) is counterbalanced by his downfall (7.4469–4545); but here the story ends quite differently, as the counterbalance to Solomon's successes is not the fall of Solomon, which is ignored, but the fall of Alexander, which had itself been largely set aside in the *Confessio* (see note to lines 36–42). Yet if we are to assume Henry's familiarity with the *Confessio* (see note to lines 24–25), we must also assume that the mention of Solomon carries with it its own intrinsic blessings and warnings. For all his own personal wisdom, despite all the gifts bestowed upon him by God, in the end Solomon fell for lack of right counsel within and without.

36–70   Six of these thirty-five lines begin with the adversative *Bot.* Having defended Henry's right to rule and further established the complete worthiness of Henry's usurpation, Gower moves quickly through a sequence of negations that serve as counterpoint to Henry's successes and a warning for his reign.

36–42   *Bot Alisaundre . . . had it of conqweste.* Alexander is clearly a negative example here (on the adversatives, see note to lines 36–70), his failure being that he was a man of the sword, one who won his lands through conquest. Forni (*Chaucerian Apocrypha*, p. 140) notes comparison with the Tale of Alexander and the Pirate (*CA* 3.2361–2480), where the difference between the conqueror and the pirate is one of degree, not kind. Even more, the tale is there utilized against the vice of Homicide, and it is followed by Genius' explication of Alexander's ignominious demise. Chaucer's Manciple uses a story of Alexander and an outlaw to similar effect (*CT* IX[H]223–39), and the comparison is even found in Augustine's *Civ. Dei* IV.4. Book 7 of the *Confessio* may seem to be more kind to Alexander, portraying the relationship between Aristotle and Alexander in a fairly benign light, but that is because we see the soon-to-be conqueror only as audience to the great teacher. Perhaps Gower hoped that the rising star of English politics, Bolingbroke, might emulate Alexander as one who appears to listen. But the comparison goes scarcely beyond that. Gower certainly did not wish for the young aristocrat to adopt the ways of the Macedonian and set about trying to conquer the world: quite to the contrary, Gower condemns Alexander repeatedly as a tyrant. The same conditions and uses of Alexander are in play here, as the poet focuses on Alexander's failures rather than his successes: as we have seen, Gower plays down the role of conquest in his praise of Henry. One reason may have been tact (see the Introduction), but Gower also hoped to see Henry as a peacemaker, as a good king ought to be (lines 70 ff.) rather than as a fool who sets out to conquer the world or become Holy Roman Emperor (as Richard had apparently desired).

45   *This sinful world was al paiene tho.* Grady argues that Gower is simply "incapable
        of condemning Alexander" here ("Lancastrian Gower," p. 563), but that is
        scarcely true. That Alexander provides the occasion for Aristotle's teaching in
        the *Confessio* is evident, but in Gower's work occasion is no guarantee of success.
        Genius teaches Amans for eight long books in the *Confessio* without the lover
        learning much at all, and Alexander throughout stands firmly as Gower's su-
        preme example of the vanity of earthly conquest (n.b. the tales of Diogenes and
        Alexander, *CA* 3.1201 ff., and Alexander and the Pirate, *CA* 3.2363 ff. — tales
        told, respectively, as exempla against Discord and Homicide). Whereas Grady
        regards the poet's shift here from Alexander himself to the mode of Alexander's
        times as one designed to obscure attention from the problem of Alexander's suc-
        cesses, akin to a magician who gestures with one hand while the other retrieves
        the card hidden in his sleeve, I rather think the shift is more specifically focused
        on explaining Alexander's results. That is, Gower does not deny that Alexander
        achieved glorious conquests. By the same token, he acknowledges that Henry,
        too, has had success. The difference is that Alexander lived in a pagan world in
        which he had little insight but to wage war. Certainly he had little precedence
        for other courses of action in achieving his ends. But the same quite clearly does
        not apply to Henry, who has "the feith of Crist" (line 50) as a model for (at the
        least) temperate behavior. The aim is not to obscure Alexander's guilt (he is
        implicitly called a tyrant in line 48), but to hold Henry to a higher standard.

49   *infortune of sinne.* The Boethian model of Fortune presented in the opening para-
        graph is here set aside (or, perhaps more properly, modified) by a more theo-
        logical consideration of the rise and fall of men. The import is that Henry is not
        a simple subject to the whim of Fortune; rather, as a Christian king (see lines
        50–52) he has the means to keep some measure of control over his own destiny by
        rightly ruling both himself and his country. Peace, not war, should be his métier.

53   *Bot yit it mot be tempred.* Here Gower, writing a poem praising peace, begins to
        provide an excuse for Henry's clearly unpeaceful actions. Pity can be tempered
        (a nice way of saying "set aside") at certain times under certain conditions. Such
        a time, he says a few lines later, was the end of Richard's reign. And such a condi-
        tion was Henry's right to the throne. See the notes to lines 56 and 57–59, below.

56   *The lawe of riht schal noght be leid aside.* The *lawe of riht* echoes across the poem in
        various ways. Fisher (*John Gower*, p. 132) sees it as a direct reminder to Henry that
        he had notified Parliament on 30 September 1399 that he would not deprive
        anyone of his or her rights as a part of his usurpation (see note to lines 57–59).
        It is not difficult, too, to see in this a reference to the vein of natural law that
        pulses so strongly through the corpus of Gower's works. More topically, however,
        the *lawe of riht* also refers to the proper laws of inheritance which Richard *leid
        aside* when he took Bolingbroke's lands and cast him into exile; after all, it was the
        disinheriting of Henry, the canceling of what was rightfully his, that most justi-
        fied, in the eyes of the realm, his precipitous return.

57–59   *So mai a kyng of werre the viage / Ordeigne . . . To cleime . . . his rightful heritage.*
        Skeat observes that this "obviously refers to Bolingbroke's invasion, when he
        came, as he said, to claim his inheritance" (7.496), and it certainly does conform

with the support that Gower gave to this claim in the opening lines of the poem (see note to line 14). Most important, however, is the fact and the means of the reference. That is, it is only here, after commending the king and then setting the broad terms of the proper workings of the world, that Gower makes mention of the conquest. And even still, the poet is oblique in his approach, presenting it as advice for any king. There is a correlation between Gower's stipulation of acceptable conquest here and Henry's "reassuring" remarks to Parliament on 30 September 1399:

> Sires, I thanke god and yow Spirituell and Temporell and alle the States off the lande. And I do yow to vndirstone that hit is nat my wille that no man thynk that by wey off conquest I wolde disherite eny man off his heritage, ffraunchises, or other Rihtes that him ouht to have, ne to putte him oute off that he hath and hath by goode lawes and custumes off the Rewme: excepte thes persones that haue ben ageyns the goode purpos and the comvne profyte off the Rewme. (*Chronicles of London*, ed. Kingsford, p. 46)

On the volumes that Henry's "excepte" speaks (and the corresponding vagueness of "thes persones"), see Grady, "Lancastrian Gower," pp. 557–58. On the law of right and its topicality as an excuse for Henry's own actions, see note to line 56, above.

61–62   *if God Himsilve wolde / Afferme love and pes betwen the kynges.* The idea is at once topical, with Gower surely having in mind the internecine conflicts of the fourteenth century (a topic he will revisit later in the poem), and also historical. In particular, Gower might well be thinking of the biblical precedent of Ephesians 2:11–22, in which Paul describes how gentiles and Jews have become of one body, as Christ brought peace to them both.

66   *For of bataile the final ende is pees.* Yeager ("Pax Poetica") rightly notes that such an opinion is Augustinian, though Grady amusingly points out that it borders on the Orwellian to modern ears ("Lancastrian Gower," p. 565).

69   *Bot if so were that he myghte chese.* The final *Bot* in the long string of adversatives beginning at line 36 (see note to lines 36–70, above) gives way to the notion of choice, which is the ultimate arbiter between the twin exempla of Solomon and Alexander as they have been presented in the poem: the former chose wisdom, the latter the sword. Gower's not-too-subtle implication is that Henry, too, faces a choice in the rule of his new-won kingdom. In Book 3 of the *Confessio*, Gower places the blame for Alexander's death on Alexander's own choices (line 2461). See Peck, *Kingship and Common Profit*, pp. 87–89, for Gower's views on fate, which "connects directly to the behavior of will" (p. 88). Peck cites parallel observations in *VC* II.iv.203–08.

70   *Betre is the pees, of which may no man lese.* Though he presumably does not fully change subject until line 106, where the first paragraph mark occurs, Gower clearly sets off the first seventy lines of the poem as a unit in and of themselves, marking the division by the internal rhymes that form a triplet of rhyme between lines 69 and 70 and put a full stop to the preceding train of thought. The

internally rhymed word, *pees*, is simultaneously established as the subject of the subsequent three stanzas.

71–72   *Sustene pes . . . to sette his liege lord in reste.* If *In Praise of Peace* was written in the last months of 1399, then these lines would have taken on deeper meaning in the succeeding years as the men of the realm most assuredly did not keep the peace in order to set their king *in reste.* Like Daniel at Belshazzar's Feast, perhaps Gower wisely saw the writing on the wall, just as he had earlier in changing the dedication of his *Confessio* to the young Bolingbroke. If so, he probably met the news of the various rebellions against Henry with a mixture of sorrow and sigh, disturbed to be right once again. Aside from this, Gower's phrase *Sustene pes* (line 71) is interesting in that it might imply that peace was the original status of Creation, a balance disturbed by the fall of the angels and of man. Lack of peace thus implies the presence of sin, a theological position that well accords, for example, with that proposed by Aquinas in *Summa Theologica* II.ii.q29.a3.

73   *these othre men.* Gower's *these* seems directed, as if he means some particular men who are not of a mind to give the same advice as the poet. While this is surely possible, it is more likely that Gower means that *most* other men do not pursue peace; thus he needs advise the king to do so.

76   *oure dedly werre cesse.* That Gower is talking directly about the long war with France and its various satellites is hardly in doubt. Though the period from the death of Edward III in 1377 to the ascension of Henry V in 1413 is often termed the "interim" period of the Hundred Years' War, it was hardly a time without conflict between the two great powers. And though tensions between England and France had remained high throughout Gower's life, Henry's military successes at home in England would have naturally raised the thought in some quarters that he might make a second move against France. Gower's negative opinion on such an idea is clear.

78   *Pes is the chief of al the worldes welthe.* Macaulay points out an echo of *CA* 3.2264–65: "pes comended, / Which is the chief of mannes welthe"; cf. *VC* VI.xiii.971.

84   *withoute Goddis sonde.* This recalls Alexander, who could not properly achieve peace given the fact that he was a pagan living in a pagan time (see note to line 45). At the same time, however, it recalls Christ, who was God's message made flesh, the God-man of the divine Word.

87   *Above alle othre good.* The term *good* does double work here, indicating that peace is better than any other possible good (idea) and any other actual good (object).

90   *Pes is of al charité the keie / Which hath the lif and soule for to weie.* Compare Aquinas, in *Summa Theologica* II.ii.q29.a3, who writes that peace "is the work of charity directly, since charity, according to its very nature, causes peace." That peace stands in judgment speaks to Christ as Prince of Peace.

95   *werre turneth into noght.* Whereas God creates out of nothing through His peace (compare line 22), war unmakes creation into nothing. Gower expresses the idea in very similar terms in *CA* 3.2273–74: "For alle thing which God hath wroght / In erthe, werre it bringth to noght."

96   *these olde bokes*. Gower presumably means books of history, which time and again
         speak of the dangers of war and the impulse to conquer. But it is difficult not to
         think that Gower is thinking more specifically of the eight books (and prologue)
         that he himself had given the king: *Confessio Amantis*, which had "essamples"
         (line 93) enough for any occasion. See the note to lines 25–26.

102–05   Gower reminds Henry of the looming and lasting threat of mortality, a threat
         for which he will provide specific examples at lines 281–87.

107–08   *It sleth the prest in Holi Chirche at Masse, / Forlith the maide and doth here flour to falle*.
         While it is tempting to see a reference here to Becket and Henry II, or Langton
         and John, such specifics are unlikely. Gower is echoing back to lines he wrote in
         the *Confessio Amantis* on the sin of homicide: "The cherche is brent, the priest is
         slain, / The wif, the maide is ek forlain" (*CA* 3.2275–76). These lines of the
         Confessio immediately precede the Tale of Alexander and the Pirate (see note to
         lines 36–42, above).

109   *werre makth the grete citee lasse*. Gower could have in mind London, or even Paris,
         but also might be thinking in Augustinian terms of the greater city in which all
         men partake.

113   *The werre bringth in poverté at hise hieles*. Macaulay hears an echo of *CA* 3.2294–95:
         "And ek thei [werres] bringen in poverte / Of worldes good, it is merveile."

115   *The werre hath set his cart on thilke whieles*. Macaulay points out an echo of *CA*
         Prol.444–45, where Gower writes about those who follow on the heels of Simon
         Magus, "Whos carte goth upon the whieles / Of coveitise and worldes Pride."
         Here Gower seems to shift the concept of the wheels quickly into a Boethian
         sphere, where Fortune (line 116) seems to dictate much of what occurs. A pun
         thereby results, warning the reader to be wary of setting his cart upon the wheels
         of Fortune.

122   *Leie to this olde sor a newe salve*. Compare Amans' supplication at the end of the
         Confessio, where Amans asks (also in rhyme royal) for salve upon the wound of
         Cupid's fiery dart (*CA* 8.2287–90). The earlier prayer, followed as it is by the
         poet's apocalyptic self-realization of identity (8.2321) and prayer for England
         (8.2971–3172), thus finds its parallel in the present poem as Gower's plea for
         healing on behalf of that same England ultimately leads to a realization of the
         country's place within the broader context of Christendom and humanity (lines
         379–85). The wounds, whether from lack of love or lack of love's cousin, pity,
         similarly stand in the way of health, security, and proper rule.

134–38   *Wher nedeth most . . . the werste is for to doute*. The *loke* of line 134 is here tied directly
         to the *se* of line 137: Henry's greatest need should be his kingdom, so it is there
         that he most needs to take care — foreign concerns must always come second to
         the communal needs that should be seen, and met without hesitation, at home.

134   *nedeth most, behoveth most*. Proverbial. See Whiting, N61.

155   *O kyng fulfild of grace and of knyghthode*. Macaulay observes that the address to
         Henry closely echoes that in the revised Prologue to the *Confessio*, which de-

scribes the future king as "Ful of knyhthode and alle grace" (*CA* Prol.89). The compliment to Henry's chivalric qualities would have met with approval from a king who liked to think himself the flower of English chivalry.

157–58   *If pes be profred unto thi manhode, / Thin honour sauf.* Macaulay points out that "Peace with honor" is a theme that appears commonly in Gower's work (e.g., *VC* VII.xxiv.1415). The question of what constitutes proper manhood comes up again at line 200, where Gower posits that while good knights should selflessly defend the Holy Church, contemporary knights are more interested in personal fame. It is interesting to note that manhood also appears once again between these parallels, at line 173, where it is in reference to Christ's acceptance of flesh, the ultimate example of humility and peace.

170–71   *Among the Ten Comandementz . . . manslaghtre schulde be forbore.* The Ten Commandments received by Moses in the theophany at Sinai were widely regarded in Christian circles as the mark of the "old" laws superseded by Christ's coming. They are listed twice in the Bible, at Exodus 20:1–17 and Deuteronomy 5:1–21.

174   *Pes was the ferste thing He let do crie.* Gower probably has in mind the Beatitudes, which are among the first teachings of Christ in the Gospel of Matthew. Specific among them for the present purpose is Matthew 5:9 "Blessed are the peacemakers, for they will be called the children of God."

176–80   *And er Crist wente out . . . He beqwath to His disciples . . . charité.* The reference is to the Last Supper, especially John 14:27: "Peace I leave with you; my peace I give to you: not as the world giveth, do I give unto you. Let not your heart be troubled, nor let it be afraid."

190–96   On wars against the pagans, see note to line 250.

197–200   *to kepe of Holy Chirche . . . stant to his manhode.* Theoretically, it was a defining characteristic of knights that they were to defend the Christian faith (see, e.g., *Piers Plowman*, where the idea of a Christ-knight becomes literal when Jesus takes up arms to joust with the Devil). Practically, however, Gower observed something less savory in contemporary knights. He accuses them here of seeking only fame (line 201). Gower also berates contemporary chivalric practices at *VC* VII.i.31–40 and in *De lucis scrutinio*, lines 49–54.

208   *Popes bulle.* Gower seems to be referring to some particular papal bull ordering Christians to make pagans "obeie" (line 209), and the two most probable originators would be Pope Boniface IX in Rome (1389–1404) or the rival Anti-pope Benedict XIII in Avignon (1394–1417). Boniface's 1394 call for a renewed crusade against the continuing Islamic threat in the East, a call that resulted in the "crusade" that ended so disastrously with the Battle of Nicopolis on 25 September 1396 (for more on which, see below, note to line 267), is one possible referent. More likely, however, are Boniface's later pleas for crusade in April 1398 and in March 1399 (see Setton, *History of the Crusades* 3.85). These calls for action ultimately went unanswered, but Gower's very present concern about them would seem to indicate that answering them was still a possibility. This topicality would thus argue for an earlier (1399–1400) dating for the composition of *In Praise of*

Peace rather than a later one (i.e., 1402–04). By 1401, it was clear that the West was more interested in internal disputes than in external ones.

216–17   *Crist bad . . . His evangile teche.* Probably a reference to the Great Commission of Matthew 28:19–20.

218   *More light it is to kepe than to make.* Proverbial. See Whiting K3; compare C518, H412, the latter of which cites Trevisa's translation of Higden (1.235[1–3]): "That this is lasse maistrie, to wynne and to conquere, than it is to kepe and to save that that is conquered and i-wonne."

225–31   *Bot thogh the Heved of Holy Chirche above . . . It lith in hem that barge for to stiere.* Gower in essence disowns the papacy to focus all the more on the responsibility of secular leaders when *Petres schip as now hath lost his stiere* (line 230). Gower's assertion of royal dominion apart from even the Roman papacy (much less that in Avignon) seems almost reform-minded, though mainly it reasserts his basic proposition that a king should rule his own land well, rather than attempting to meddle in foreign policies (see *CA* 8.2109–20).

250   *Sarazins.* Gower might seem at odds with himself about what one should do with the Saracens, since in the *Confessio Amantis* he gives the opposite advice: "A Sarazin if I sle schal, / I sle the Soule forth withal, / And that was nevere Cristes lore" (*CA* 4.1679–81; compare, too, 3.2481–2546). Similarly, his discussion of Homicide in *CA* 3.2251–2360 is absolute in its condemnation of killing. Yet, as here, Gower blames the pagans for much of the world's unrest in *De lucis scrutinio*, line 33. Even so, "Let men ben armed agein hem to fighte" (line 251) should not be equated with advocacy of crusades or wholesale bloodshed; rather, it justifies defense. Gower is thus in no way advocating Henry to war, whether it is against France or the East. Peace is his goal from beginning to end in this poem.

251–52   *fighte / . . . knyht . . . righte.* Just as he did at lines 69–70 (see note to line 70), Gower rounds off a section of his discussion with a slightly more complex internal rhyme scheme.

254   *Holy Cherche is in hersilf divided.* Gower refers to the Great Schism, which had begun in 1378 when French cardinals, upset at the actions of the Italian Pope Urban VI in Rome, elected Clement VII to a rival papal seat in Avignon. The result was a split within the Catholic Church, as the two halves of Cristendom each excommunicated the other and set off a series of internecine conflicts, many of which underscored the tensions between England and France in particular. Gower finds the schism directly responsible for the rise of the heresy of Lollardy; see, e.g., *De lucis scrutinio*, lines 4 ff., and *CA* Prol.328–51, where he writes: "Scisme causeth for to bringe / This newe secte of Lollardie" (lines 348–49). Lollardy becomes an essential part of the "plague" which is destroying England in Gower's *Carmen super multiplici viciorum pestilencia*.

258–59   *reule / . . . reule.* Gower often uses *rime riche* to emphasize ideas, as he does here. Perfected in *MO*, the technique (in which two homophones are used as the rhyme words in a couplet) is utilized extensively in *CA* (e.g., 5.79–90, where Gower uses a number in a row — see Olsen, "*Betwene Ernest and Game,*" pp. 55–56). For general discussion of the technique in Gower, see Itô, "Gower's Use of Rime Riche." Here, Gower deftly uses the homophones to reveal part of his argument in microcosm, as "rule" (*reule*, line 258) leads to "order" (*reule*, line 259).

260   On the metaphor of the body politic, compare *O deus immense*, line 85. Here, the metaphor is prepared in line 167. For a study of the body as microcosm of creation, see Barkan, *Nature's Work of Art*.

267   *The two defaltes bringen in the thridde.* That is, Christendom is doubly divided: by the Great Schism and by its own internal conflicts. These double faults have brought upon a third: the Saracen threat. The Ottoman Empire had started its incursions into the West in the middle of the fourteenth century, commencing a series of battles in the Balkans as it pushed back against the shrinking Byzantine Empire (little more than Constantinople and Thessalonica by 1400) and the kingdoms grown in its wake. After a resounding Ottoman victory at Kosovo in 1389, only Hungary remained as a substantial buffer between old Europe and the rising Islamic tide. Calls for crusade soon followed, with negotiations between Richard II in England, Charles VI in France, and Sigismund in Hungary. Though a sizable English force under the command of John of Gaunt had originally been intended to take part, the final English contribution was probably only a thousand men. These joined with Burgundian, Bavarian, and Hungarian forces to mount an army some one hundred thousand strong which marched on Nicopolis, plundering on the way. The Ottoman Sultan Bayezid I met them there and cut the impatient crusaders to ribbons in a tactical ambush. Bayezid beheaded several thousand of the captive crusaders. Nicopolis would seem to be the last gasp of the crusades, as the West never again mounted any sizable expedition despite further papal calls for action (see the note to line 208). And England and France quickly turned to fighting each other once more. Whether "the dedly werre" that Gower refers to in line 271 is Nicopolis or the renewed spirit of cross-Channel conflict that arose in its wake is unclear; compare line 76 and note.

274–75 *My worthi noble prince and kyng enoignt, / Whom God hath of His grace so preserved.* Gower's laudatory formulas, emphasizing his definition of a good king as one who is worthy, noble, and blessed by God, echoes back to the opening sequences of the poem. Also of note here, however, is the reference to the king's sacred anointing, something that would carry particular weight for Henry: the new king was so concerned about this aspect of his legitimacy that the Lancastrians claimed that the oil of anointment at his coronation was the legendary oil that had been given to Thomas à Becket by the Virgin Mary and intended for a coming king of great worth (see *H. aquile pullus*, line 3, and *O recolende*, line 9).

281–83 *Alisandre . . . Arthus.* These are the nine worthies of medieval convention. Note, however, that the typical religious differentiation between them is not given here; they are not identified as pagans (Alexander, Hector, Caesar), Jews (Judas, David, Joshua), and Christians (Charlemagne, Godfrey, Arthur). Instead, they are presented as nine men who are united in their equality before the ultimate scythe of death (lines 284–87). That their fame abides is thus an exemplum of their futile vanity (line 285), a model to be feared, not followed.

291   *ther ben the marches save.* A fine example of Gower's perpetual concern with borders, boundaries, and definition, where erosion and decay so often subvert the substance of dominion. Absolutes, both moral and political, are most revealed by their edges.

295–96 *Of the tenetz to winne or lese a chace / Mai no lif wite er that the bal be ronne.* Gower moves quite abruptly from the broad themes of moral ideas to a concrete exemplum from domestic life. On the metaphor, which is the first known use of the word *tennis* in the English language according to the *OED* (though hardly the first reference to the game — compare Chaucer *TC* 4.460), Macaulay explains: "The question of winning a 'chase' at tennis is not one which is decided at once by the stroke that is made, but depends on later developments" (554). It is interesting to note that tennis was largely considered an invention of the French during the Middle Ages.

297–98 *Al stant in God . . . that it be begonne.* Just as quickly as he moved to the domestic example of a tennis game, Gower moves to the level of the divine. At one level, the theological discussion of these two lines is a natural extension of the tennis metaphor: though the tennis players may not know the outcome of the game, God knows the outcome of the game as well as the trajectory of each individual shot. Beyond this, however, the sudden shifts from domestic to divine (and back again in the next two lines) reveals that the workings in each are differences in degree, not kind; what is applicable to the microcosm applies to the macrocosm.

299–301 *Men sein the wolle . . . be durable.* Having moved from the domestic example of tennis to the large-scale perspective of God, Gower moves back again to the domestic in discussing the making of good cloth. Like tennis, in which a "successful game is built on a foresightful strategy in the early going," "strong durable cloth depends on the proper treatment of its raw material, well-spun wool" (Grady, "Lancastrian Gower," pp. 567–68). As Grady notes, these examples constitute a "neo-Boethian admonition" to Henry that he should "prepare warily and carefully for a world ruled by Fortune" (p. 568). And for Gower in this poem, of course, the best means of preparation is to choose rule by peace. The choice of wool in this proverbial advice is surely no accident, either, as the wool trade was the axle upon which the wheel of the late medieval English economy turned. The exterior fate of England, most assuredly seen in its trade economics, is irrevocably bound up with its internal fate. If Henry rules well within (preparing *wel sponne* wool), then England will do well without (like *durable* cloth that is *strong* and, in so many ways, *profitable*).

319–22 *weie: / . . . weie, / . . . wise, / . . . wise.* Gower's placement of two *rime riches* back to back calls particular attention to these lines in which he argues that the only sure "way" (*weie*, line 319) is to see that your conscience is "weighed" (*weie*, line 320) and that you use "wisdom" (*wise*, line 321) in all your "ways" (*wise*, line 322).

323–24 *Th'apostle seith . . . charité.* See Paul, in 1 Corinthians 13:1–13, where the apostle discusses the gift of love (Lat. *caritas*); Paul begins: "If I speak with the tongues of men, and of angels, and have not charity, I am become as sounding brass."

327   *thilke vertu which is seid pité.* This stands against Aquinas who, in *Summa Theologica* II.ii.q29.a4, argues that "virtue is not the last end, but the way thereto. But peace is the last end, in a sense, as Augustine says (*De Civ. Dei* xix.11). Therefore peace is not a virtue."

330–31 *Cassodre . . . Seith, wher that pité regneth, ther is grace.* I.e., Cassiodorus (ca. 490–583), a one-time powerful Roman statesman who established the monastery of Vivarium on his own estate and took orders himself. He translated and edited the Bible in various forms, began a school of critical scribes, and wrote a number of books of his own, including *Institutiones divinarum et saecularium litterarum* (which establishes a plan of biblical study for the scribes at his monastery), *Historia tripartita* (an ecclesiastical history from the combined writings of Theodoret, Sozomen, and Socrates), and *Variarum*. The latter, a collection of his letters, some short writings, and even some bits of philosophy, was strangely popular. Chaucer uses it six times in his Tale of Melibee (*CT* VII[B²]1196, using *Variarum* 10.18; 1348, using 1.17; 1438, using 1.4; 1528, using 1.30; 1564, using 2.13; 1642, using 1.4); on Melibee as a poem advising Richard on behalf of peace, see Stillwell, "Political Meaning," and Scattergood, "Chaucer and the French War." Gower seems here to be quoting *Variarum* 11.40, "pietas est, quae regit et caelos," which he also utilizes in *CA* 7.3161–62*: "Cassiodore in his aprise telleth, / 'The regne is sauf, where pité dwelleth.'" For more on Cassiodorus, see Jones, "Influence of Cassiodorus."

337–57 *To se what pité . . . be preised evermore.* Compare Gower's earlier Tale of Constantine and Silvester (*CA* 2.3187–3496), which is given as an example of how Charity, "the moder of Pité" (2.3174), stands against the vice of Envy (for discussion of the *Confessio* text, see Olsson, *John Gower and the Structures of Conversion*, pp. 102–06). Grady notes that "once again some of the details of the *Confessio*'s version have been suppressed." In this shorter version, for example, Constantine no longer needs to hear the cries of the infants and their mothers in order to feel pity. And, even more interesting, the account here mentions neither Constantine's earlier role as "fo to Cristes lay" (2.3354), nor the fact that the conversion of all Rome occurred on "peine of deth" (2.3469), nor that the earlier story ends with an angelic pronouncement cursing Constantine's Donation to the papacy (2.3490–92). As with the earlier "sanitized" account of Solomon, we probably ought not to see Gower as stumbling through his sources here. Quite to the contrary, Gower surely anticipates Henry's awareness of Constantine's faults. They need not be elucidated. Solomon did well, only to end badly. So, too, with Constantine. Gower dwells on the positives in their stories because Henry has, so far, done well. The ending of the king's story, however, has not yet been written.

339   *Constantin.* Constantine the Great; see the note to lines 337–57.

365–78 *My lord . . . In worschipe of thi sceptre and of thi throne.* These two stanzas bring the poem full circle, as Gower returns to the lauds and approbation with which he had commenced his *lettre* (line 375). The poet makes the circularity clear in repeating key words and phrases between the opening and closing stanzas: e.g., "worschipe" (lines 5, 378), and "every man is holde" (lines 7, 373). This movement back to the beginning point sets the stage for the final stanza, in which Gower turns from England to Christendom; see note to lines 379–85.

365–66   *My lord, in whom hath ever yit be founde / Pité withoute spot of violence.* Gower's praise of Henry IV is a revision of praise he had given to Richard II in the First Recension of *CA*: "In whom hath evere yit be founde / Justice medled with pité" (8.2988–89*). This is not the only instance of Gower's revising praise for the earlier king in order to apply it to the latter. The poem *Rex celi deus*, which follows *In Praise of Peace* in the Trentham MS, does the same — e.g., *Rex celi deus*, line 39, asks Henry to establish peace, using lines originally from *VC* VI.xviii.1179*, which were addressed to Richard. Gower might well have expected Henry to be aware of this kind of literally revisionist history; indeed, the poet's concern with good kingship posits that the same basic choices are ultimately set before all kings: it is how they make their way among those choices that determines their fate. Henry, to his benefit, is thus at an advantage over Richard not necessarily because of any greater personal qualifications for sovereignty, but because he has, at the very least, the good fortune of knowing Richard's past choices and their sometimes disastrous outcomes. Kings, in other words, are by nature interchangeable, an opinion that Henry no doubt needed simultaneously to accept and fear.

379–85   *Noght only to my king . . . so the pes schal stonde.* Gower moves from addressing Henry to all the princes of Christendom. By thus broadening his scope after bringing this subtle poem full circle (see note to lines 365–78), Gower reveals that his advice should not be viewed as particular to the present king or present moment alone; his is a system of ethics, whether viewed piecemeal or across the whole of his writing career, that is meant to be natural to man. His concern is, and has always been, less with Henry than with the "worschipe of thi sceptre and of thi throne" (line 378). That is, Gower is focused on the institution of kingship, not the individual king (compare *CA* 7.1751–74, where Gower remarks on the crown as symbol for proper rule). Gower's voice may indeed be a voice crying out in the wilderness — but that is its virtue and its strength. The movement from England to Christendom thus parallels Gower's movement from self-absorption to a prayer for England at the conclusion of the *Confessio Amantis*; in both the movement is one that reveals a new, more universal human experience whose macrocosmic implications are always rooted in the individual microcosm.

In *De lucis scrutinio*, lines 29–30, Gower similarly suggests that the Christian kings, lacking a papal head to unite them, must unite themselves. Compare, too, the note to lines 225–31, above.

380   *these othre princes Cristene alle.* Skeat notes: "viz. in particular, Charles VI, king of France, and Robert III, king of Scotland" (7.498).

383   *Sette ek the rightful pope uppon his stalle.* Gower does not specify who such a person would be (see the note to line 254, on the Great Schism), though he is elsewhere clear in his support of the Roman claim over the French. See, for example, the Latin marginalia to *CA* Prol.194–99, where Gower names names and casts his lot squarely with Rome. In *De lucis scrutinio*, lines 27–28, Gower complains that the

world is so far fallen that the rightful pope is not chosen by the will of God, but of men. This detraction is here posed as optimism: men must work together in order to fulfill the will of God and hold but one vicar over the Christian Church.

TEXTUAL NOTES

ABBREVIATIONS: See p. 55, above.

27   *whiche.* So MS. Mac: *which,* from Thynne.
35   *into.* So MS. Mac: *unto,* from Thynne.
39   *it.* MS: *itt,* with the second *t* canceled.
71   *Sustene.* So Mac. MS: *S,* followed by an erasure. Thynne reads *To stere.*
89   *ever.* So MS, Thynne. Mac: *evere.*
90   *al.* So MS, Thynne. Mac: *alle.*
108   *here.* So MS. Mac: *hire,* from Thynne.
122   *Leie.* So MS. Mac: *ley,* from Thynne.
126   *ever.* So MS, Thynne. Mac: *evere.*
127   *ever.* So MS, Thynne. Mac: *evere.*
129   *Lete.* So MS. Thynne: *Lette.* Mac: *Let.*
130   *putte.* So MS. Mac: *put,* from Thynne.
162   *thenke.* So MS. Thynne: *thynke.* Mac: *thenk.*
169   The larger initial here is unnoted by Mac.
181   *never.* So MS, Thynne. Mac: *nevere.*
229   *redresce.* So MS. Mac: *redresse,* from Thynne.
241   *ever.* So MS, Thynne. Mac: *evere.*
254   *hersilf.* So MS. Thynne: *herselfe.* Mac: *hirsilf.*
263   *helpples.* So MS. Thynne: *helplesse.* Mac: *helpeles.*
265   *sleth.* So MS. Mac: *sleeth,* from Thynne.
269   *Betwene.* So MS, Thynne. Mac: *betwen.*
272   *Kyng.* So MS. Mac: *King,* from Thynne.
276   *Beholde.* So MS, Thynne. Mac: *behold.*
301   *never.* So MS, Thynne. Mac: *nevere.*
329   *here.* So MS. Thynne: *her.* Mac: *hire.*
331   *regneth.* So MS. Mac: *reigneth,* from Thynne.
336   *weie.* So MS, Mac. Thynne: *way.*
342   *crualté.* A later hand has inserted a *y* between the *t* and *e.*
350   *forever.* So MS, Thynne. Mac: *forevere.*
356   *were.* So MS, Thynne. Mac: *weren.*
364   *schal.* So MS. Mac: *shal,* from Thynne.
365   *ever.* So MS, Thynne. Mac: *evere.*
384   *draughe.* So MS. Mac: *draugh,* from Thynne.

SELECT BIBLIOGRAPHY

Alan of Lille. *De Planctu Naturae.* Ed. Nikolaus M. Häring. In "Alan of Lille, 'De planctu Naturae.'" *Studi medievali,* third series 19 (1978), 797–879.

"Annales Ricardi Secundi." Johannis de Trokelowe *et anon.* In *Chronica et Annales,* 199–239. Ed. H. T. Riley. Rolls Series. London: HMSO, 1866.

Aquinas, Thomas. *Summa Theologica, Basic Writings of Saint Thomas Aquinas.* 2 vols. Ed. Anton C. Pegis. New York: Random House, 1945.

Arvanigian, Mark. "Henry IV, the Northern Nobility and the Consolidation of the Regime." In Dodd and Biggs. Pp. 117–37.

Aston, Margaret. *Lollards and Reformers: Images and Literacy in Late Medieval Religion.* London: Hambledon Press, 1984.

Baker, David J. *Between Nations: Shakespeare, Spenser, Marvell, and the Question of Britain.* Stanford, CA: Stanford University Press, 1997.

Barkan, Leonard. *Nature's Work of Art: The Human Body as Image of the World.* New Haven, CT: Yale University Press, 1975.

Bates, Robin E. "'The Queene is Defrauded of the Intent of the Law': Spenser's Advocation of Civil Law in *A View of the State of Ireland.*" *Papers on Language and Literature* 41 (2005), 123–45.

Beichner, Paul E. "Gower's Use of the *Aurora* in the *Vox Clamantis.*" *Speculum* 30 (1955), 582–95.

Bennett, Michael. "Henry of Bolingbroke and the Revolution of 1399." In Dodd and Biggs. Pp. 9–33.

Bloomfield, Morton W. *The Seven Deadly Sins: An Introduction to the History of a Religious Concept, with Special Reference to Medieval English Literature.* East Lansing: Michigan State University Press, 1967.

Boethius. *Boethii Philosophiae Consolatio.* Ed. Ludovicus Bieler. Corpus Christianorum, ser. lat. XCIV. Turnhout: Brepols, 1957.

Carlson, David R. "Gower's Early Latin Poetry: Text-Genetic Hypotheses of an *Epistola ad regem* (ca. 1377–1380) from the Evidence of John Bale." *Mediaeval Studies* 65 (2003), 293–317.

———. "The Invention of the Anglo-Latin Public Poetry (circa 1367–1402) and Its Prosody, Especially in John Gower." *Mittellateinisches Jahrbuch* 39 (2004), 389–406.

———. "A Rhyme Distribution Chronology of John Gower's Latin Poetry." *Studies in Philology* (forthcoming).

Chaucer, Geoffrey. *The Riverside Chaucer.* Gen. ed. Larry D. Benson. Third ed. Boston, MA: Houghton-Mifflin, 1987.

Chronicles of London. Ed. C. L. Kingsford. London: Alan Sutton, 1977.

Chronicon Angliae auctore monacho quondam Sancti Albani. Ed. E. M. Thompson. Rolls Series. London: HMSO, 1874.

Coffman, George R. "John Gower in His Most Significant Role." In *Elizabethan Studies and Other Essays in Honor of George F. Reynolds.* University of Colorado Studies Series B, II.4. Boulder: University of Colorado Press, 1945. Pp. 52–61.

———. "John Gower, Mentor for Royalty: Richard II." *PMLA* 69 (1954), 953–64.

Dante Alighieri. *The Divine Comedy.* Ed. Charles S. Singleton. 6 vols. Bolingen Series LXXX. Princeton, NJ: Princeton University Press, 1970–75.

Delasanta, Rodney. "Chaucer and Strode." *Chaucer Review* 26 (1991), 205–18.

Dodd, Gwilym, and Douglas Biggs, eds. *Henry IV: The Establishment of the Regime, 1399–1406*. Wood-bridge, UK: York Medieval Press, 2003.

Echard, Siân. "With Carmen's Help: Latin Authorities in the *Confessio Amantis*." *Studies in Philology* 95 (1998), 1–40.

———. "Designs for Reading: Some Manuscripts of Gower's *Confessio Amantis*." *Trivium* 31 (1999), 59–72.

———. "Gower's Books of Latin: Language, Politics and Poetry." *Studies in the Age of Chaucer* 25 (2003), 123–56.

———. "Last Words: Latin at the End of the *Confessio Amantis*." In *Interstices: Studies in Middle English and Anglo-Latin Texts in Honour of A. G. Rigg*. Ed. Richard Firth Green and Linne Mooney. Toronto: University of Toronto Press, 2004. Pp. 99–121.

———, ed. *A Companion to Gower*. Cambridge, D.S. Brewer, 2004.

———. "Gower in Print." In Echard, *Companion to Gower*. Pp. 115–35.

Echard, Siân, and Claire Fanger. *The Latin Verses in the Confessio Amantis: An Annotated Translation*, with an introduction by A. G. Rigg. East Lansing, MI: Colleagues Press, 1991.

Ferster, Judith. *Fictions of Advice: The Literature and Politics of Counsel in Late Medieval England*. Philadelphia: University of Pennsylvania Press, 1996.

Fisher, John H. *John Gower: Moral Philosopher and Friend of Chaucer*. New York: New York University Press, 1964.

Forni, Kathleen, ed. *The Chaucerian Apocrypha: A Selection*. Kalamazoo, MI: Medieval Institute Publications, 2005.

Geoffrey of Monmouth. *Historia regum Britannie of Geoffrey of Monmouth, I: Bern Burgerbibliothek, MS 568*. Ed. Neil Wright. Cambridge: D.S. Brewer, 1984.

Gower, John. *The Complete Works of John Gower*. Ed. G. C. Macaulay. 4 vols. Oxford: Clarendon Press, 1899–1902. Vols. 2 and 3 rpt. as *The English Works of John Gower*. EETS e.s. 81–82. London: K. Paul, Trench, Trubner and Co., Ltd., 1900–01; rpt. Oxford University Press 1957, 1969. [Vol. 1 is the French works; vol. 4 is the Latin works.]

———. *Confessio Amantis*. Ed. Peck. [See also *The Complete Works*, ed. Macaulay.]

———. *Cronica Tripertita*. See *The Complete Works*, ed. Macaulay. [Trans. Stockton, *Major Latin Works of John Gower*.]

———. *In Praise of Peace*. In *The Complete Works of Geoffrey Chaucer*. 7 vols. Ed. Walter W. Skeat. 7.205–16. [Skeat includes *In Praise of Peace* in the final volume, *Chaucerian and Other Pieces*.]

———. *In Praise of Peace*. See *The Complete Works*, ed. Macaulay.

———. *In Praise of Peace*. See Forni, ed., *The Chaucerian Apocrypha*.

———. *Mirour de l'Omme*. See *The Complete Works*, ed. Macaulay.

———. *Vox Clamantis*. See *The Complete Works*, ed. Macaulay. [Trans. Stockton, *Major Latin Works of John Gower*.]

Grady, Frank. "The Lancastrian Gower and the Limits of Exemplarity." *Speculum* 70 (1995), 552–75.

Green, Richard Firth. *Poets and Princepleasers: Literature and the English Court in the Late Middle Ages*. Toronto: University of Toronto Press, 1980.

———. *A Crisis of Truth: Literature and Law in Ricardian England*. Philadelphia: University of Pennsylvania Press, 1999.

Hines, John, Nathalie Cohen, and Simon Roffey. "*Iohannes Gower, Armiger, Poeta*: Records and Memorials of His Life and Death." In Echard, *Companion to Gower*. Pp. 23–42.

Hoccleve, Thomas. *The Regiment of Princes*. Ed. Charles R. Blyth. Kalamazoo, MI: Medieval Institute Publications, 1999.

Horace. *Satires, Epistles and Ars Poetica*. Ed. and trans. H. Rushton Fairclough. Loeb Classical Library. New York: Heinemann, 1926.

Isidore of Seville. *Isidori Hispalensis Episcopi: Etymologiarum sive originum*. Ed. W. M. Lindsay. 2 vols. Oxford: Clarendon Press, 1911.

Itô, Masayoshi. "Gower's Use of Rime Riche in the *Confessio Amantis*, as Compared with His Practice in the *Mirour de l'Omme* and with the Case of Chaucer." *Studies in English Literature* (English Literature Society of Japan) 46 (1969), 29–44.

———. *John Gower, the Medieval Poet*. Tokyo: Shinozaki Shorin, 1976.

John of Salisbury. *Policraticus. Ioannis Saresberiensis.* Ed. K. S. B. Keats-Rohan. Corpus Christianorum, continuatio mediaevalis CXVIII. Turnhout: Brepols, 1993.

Jones, Leslie W. "The Influence of Cassiodorus on Medieval Culture." *Speculum* 20 (1945), 433–42.

Jones, Terry, R. F. Yeager, Terry Dolan, Alan Fletcher, and Juliette Dor. *Who Murdered Chaucer? A Medieval Mystery*. London: Methuen, 2004.

Kelly, Henry Ansgar. *Love and Marriage in the Age of Chaucer*. Ithaca, NY: Cornell University Press, 1975.

King, Andy. "'They have the Hertes of the People by North': Northumberland, the Percies and Henry IV, 1399–1408." In Dodd and Biggs. Pp. 139–59.

Kirby, J. L. *Henry IV of England*. London: Constable, 1970.

Kolve, V. A. *Chaucer and the Imagery of Narrative: The First Five Canterbury Tales*. Stanford, CA: Stanford University Press, 1984.

Langland, William. *Piers Plowman: The B Version: Will's Vision of Piers Plowman, Do-Well, Do-Better, Do-Best*. Ed. George Kane and E. Talbot Donaldson. London: University of London, Athlone Press, 1975.

Marsilius of Padua. *Defensor Pacis*. Ed. Richard Scholz. In *Fontes juris Germanici antiqui, Monumenta Germaniae historica* 7. Hanover: Hahn, 1932.

McKenna, John W. "The Coronation Oil of the Yorkist Kings." *English Historical Review* 82 (1967), 102–04.

Medieval Latin: An Introduction and Bibliographical Guide. Ed. F. A. C. Mantello and A. G. Rigg. Washington, DC: Catholic University of America Press, 1996; rpt. 1999.

Mum and the Sothsegger. In *Richard the Redeless and Mum and the Sothsegger*. Ed. James M. Dean. Kalamazoo, MI: Medieval Institute Publications, 2000.

Neville, Cynthia J. "Scotland, the Percies and the Law in 1400." In Dodd and Biggs. Pp. 73–93.

Nicholson, Peter. "The Dedications of Gower's *Confessio Amantis*." *Mediaevalia* 10 (1984), 159–80.

Olsen, Alexandra Hennessey. *"Betwene Ernest and Game": The Literary Artistry of the Confessio Amantis*. Bern: Peter Lang, 1990.

Olsson, Kurt. *John Gower and the Structures of Conversion: A Reading of the Confessio Amantis*. Publications of the John Gower Society 4. Cambridge: D. S. Brewer, 1992.

Patch, Howard Rollin. *The Goddess Fortuna*. Cambridge, MA: Harvard University Press, 1927. Rpt. New York: Octagon Books, 1974.

Pearsall, Derek. "Gower's Latin in the *Confessio Amantis*." In *Latin and Vernacular: Studies in Late-Medieval Texts and Manuscripts*. Ed. A. J. Minnis. Cambridge: D. S. Brewer, 1989. Pp. 13–25.

———. "The Organisation of the Latin Apparatus in Gower's *Confessio Amantis*: The Scribes and Their Problems." In *The Medieval Book and a Modern Collector: Essays in Honour of Toshiyuki Takamiya*. Ed. Takami Matsuda, Richard A. Linenthal, and John Scahill. Cambridge: D. S. Brewer, 2004. Pp. 99–112.

Peck, Russell A. *Kingship and Common Profit in Gower's Confessio Amantis*. Carbondale: Southern Illinois University Press, 1978.

———. "Number as Cosmic Language." In *Essays in the Numerical Criticism of Medieval Literature*. Ed. Caroline D. Eckhardt. Lewisburg, PA: Bucknell University Press, 1980.

———, ed. *Confessio Amantis*. 3 vols. Kalamazoo, MI: Medieval Institute Publications, 2000–04.

———. "The Politics and Psychology of Governance in Gower: Ideas of Kingship and Real Kings." In Echard, *Companion to Gower*. Pp. 215–38.

———. "John Gower: Editor, Strong Reader, and Ethical Geometrician." In *John Gower: Manuscripts, Readers, Contexts*. Ed. Malte Urban and Georgiana Donavin. Turnhout: Brepols, forthcoming.

Raby, F. J. E. *A History of Secular Latin Poetry in the Middle Ages*. 2 vols. Oxford: Clarendon Press, 1934.

Rigg, A. G. *A History of Anglo-Latin Literature 1066–1422*. Cambridge: Cambridge University Press, 1992.

———. "Anglo-Latin in the Ricardian Age." In *Essays on Ricardian Literature in Honour of J. A. Burrow*. Ed. A. J. Minnis, Charlotte C. Morse, and Thorlac Turville-Petre. Oxford: Clarendon Press, 1997. Pp. 121–41.

Rigg, A. G., and Edward S. Moore. "The Latin Works: Politics, Lament, Praise." In Echard, *Companion to Gower*. Pp. 153–64.

Rotuli Parliamentorum. Ed. J. Strachey. 6 vols. London: House of Lords, 1767–83.

Saul, Nigel. *Richard II*. New Haven, CT: Yale University Press, 1997.

Scattergood, V. J. "Chaucer and the French War: *Sir Thopas* and *Melibee*." In *Court and Poet: Selected Proceedings of the International Courtly Literature Society [Liverpool 1980]*. Ed. Glyn S. Burgess. Liverpool: Francis Cairns, 1981. Pp. 287–96.

Setton, Kenneth Meyer, gen. ed. *A History of the Crusades*. Second ed. 6 vols. Madison: University of Wisconsin Press, 1969–89.

Stillwell, Gardiner. "The Political Meaning of Chaucer's Tale of Melibee." *Speculum* 19 (1944), 433–44.

Stockton, Eric W., trans. *The Major Latin Works of John Gower*. Seattle: University of Washington Press, 1962.

Strohm, Paul. *Hochon's Arrow: The Social Imagination of Fourteenth-Century Texts*. Princeton, NJ: Princeton University Press, 1992.

———. *England's Empty Throne: Usurpation and the Language of Legitimation, 1399–1422*. New Haven, CT: Yale University Press, 1998.

Tuck, Anthony. "Henry IV and Chivalry." In Dodd and Biggs. Pp. 55–71.

Usk, Adam. *Chronicon de Adae de Usk AD 1377–1421*. Ed. E. M. Thompson. Second ed. London: Frowde, 1904.

———. *The Chronicle of Adam Usk 1377–1421*. Ed. and trans. Chris Given-Wilson. Oxford: Clarendon Press, 1997.

Virgil. *Virgil*. Ed. and trans. H. Rushton Fairclough, rev. G. P. Goold. 2 vols. I: *Eclogues, Georgics, Aeneid I–VI*; II: *Aeneid VII–XII*. Loeb Classical Library. Cambridge, MA: Harvard University Press, 1999, 2000.

Walsingham, Thomas. *Chronica Monasterii S. Albani. Thomae Walsingham quondam Monachi S. Albani, Historia Anglicana*. Vol. I, AD 1272–1381; Vol. II, 1381–1422. Ed. H. T. Riley. Rolls Series. London: Longman, Green, Longman, Roberts and Green, 1863–64.

———. *Chronica maiora*. Ed. and trans. John Taylor, et al. Vol. I. Oxford: Clarendon Press, 2003.

Wetherbee, Winthrop. "Latin Structure and Vernacular Space: Gower, Chaucer and the Boethian Tradition." In Yeager, *Chaucer and Gower*. Pp. 7–35.

White, Hugh. *Nature, Sex, and Goodness in a Medieval Literary Tradition*. Oxford: Oxford University Press, 2000.

Whiting, Bartlett Jere, with the collaboration of Helen Wescott Whiting. *Proverbs, Sentences, and Proverbial Phrases from English Writings Mainly before 1500*. Cambridge, MA: The Belknap Press of Harvard University Press, 1968.

Workman, Herbert B. *John Wyclif: A Study of the English Medieval Church*. Oxford: Clarendon Press, 1926. Rpt. Hamden, CT: Archon Books, 1966.

Yeager, R. F. "English, Latin and the Text as 'Other': The Page as Sign in the Work of John Gower." *Text: Transactions of the Society for Textual Scholarship* 3 (1987), 251–67.

———. "*Pax Poetica*: On the Pacifism of Chaucer and Gower." *Studies in the Age of Chaucer* 9 (1987), 97–121.

———. "Did Gower Write Cento?" In *John Gower: Recent Readings*. Ed. R. F. Yeager. Kalamazoo, MI: Medieval Institute Publications, 1989. Pp. 113–32.

———. *John Gower's Poetic: The Search for a New Arion*. Cambridge: D. S. Brewer, 1990.

———, ed. *Chaucer and Gower: Difference, Mutuality, Exchange*. Victoria, BC: University of Victoria Press, 1991.

———. "Learning to Speak in Tongues: Writing Poetry for a Trilingual Culture." In Yeager, *Chaucer and Gower*. Pp. 115–29.

———. "The Body Politic and the Politics of Bodies in the Poetry of John Gower." In *The Body and the Soul in Medieval Literature*. Ed. Anna Torti and Piero Boitani. Cambridge: D. S. Brewer, 1999. Pp. 145–65.

———. "John Gower's Audience: The Ballades." *Chaucer Review* 40 (2005), 81–105.

———. "Begging, or Begging Off: Chaucer's 'To His Purse.'" *Viator* 37 (2005, forthcoming).

———. "Gower in Winter: The Late Latin Poems." *Medium Aevum* (forthcoming).

Zarins, Kim. "From Head to Foot: Syllabic Play and Metamorphosis in Book I of Gower's *Vox Clamantis*." In *John Gower's Poetry: Essays at the Millennium*. Ed. R. F. Yeager. Kalamazoo, MI: Medieval Institute Publications, forthcoming.

MIDDLE ENGLISH TEXTS SERIES

The Floure and the Leafe, The Assembly of Ladies, The Isle of Ladies, edited by Derek Pearsall (1990)

Three Middle English Charlemagne Romances, edited by Alan Lupack (1990)

Six Ecclesiastical Satires, edited by James M. Dean (1991)

Heroic Women from the Old Testament in Middle English Verse, edited by Russell A. Peck (1991)

The Canterbury Tales: Fifteenth-Century Continuations and Additions, edited by John M. Bowers (1992)

Gavin Douglas, *The Palis of Honoure*, edited by David Parkinson (1992)

Wynnere and Wastoure and The Parlement of the Thre Ages, edited by Warren Ginsberg (1992)

The Shewings of Julian of Norwich, edited by Georgia Ronan Crampton (1994)

King Arthur's Death: The Middle English Stanzaic Morte Arthur and Alliterative Morte Arthure, edited by Larry D. Benson, revised by Edward E. Foster (1994)

Lancelot of the Laik and Sir Tristrem, edited by Alan Lupack (1994)

Sir Gawain: Eleven Romances and Tales, edited by Thomas Hahn (1995)

The Middle English Breton Lays, edited by Anne Laskaya and Eve Salisbury (1995)

Sir Perceval of Galles and Ywain and Gawain, edited by Mary Flowers Braswell (1995)

Four Middle English Romances: Sir Isumbras, Octavian, Sir Eglamour of Artois, Sir Tryamour, edited by Harriet Hudson (1996)

The Poems of Laurence Minot 1333–1352, edited by Richard H. Osberg (1996)

Medieval English Political Writings, edited by James M. Dean (1996)

The Book of Margery Kempe, edited by Lynn Staley (1996)

Amis and Amiloun, Robert of Cisyle, and Sir Amadace, edited by Edward E. Foster (1997)

The Cloud of Unknowing, edited by Patrick J. Gallacher (1997)

Robin Hood and Other Outlaw Tales, edited by Stephen Knight and Thomas Ohlgren (1997); second edition (2000)

The Poems of Robert Henryson, edited by Robert L. Kindrick with assistance of Kristie A. Bixby (1997)

Moral Love Songs and Laments, edited by Susanna Greer Fein (1998)

John Lydgate, *Troy Book Selections*, edited by Robert R. Edwards (1998)

Thomas Usk, *The Testament of Love*, edited by R. Allen Shoaf (1998)

Prose Merlin, edited by John Conlee (1998)

Middle English Marian Lyrics, edited by Karen Saupe (1998)

John Metham, *Amoryus and Cleopes*, edited by Stephen F. Page (1999)

Four Romances of England: King Horn, Havelok the Dane, Bevis of Hampton, Athelston, edited by Ronald B. Herzman, Graham Drake, and Eve Salisbury (1999)

The Assembly of Gods: Le Assemble de Dyeus, or Banquet of Gods and Goddesses, with the Discourse of Reason and Sensuality, edited by Jane Chance (1999)

Thomas Hoccleve, *The Regiment of Princes*, edited by Charles R. Blyth (1999)

John Capgrave, *The Life of Saint Katherine*, edited by Karen A. Winstead (1999)

John Gower, *Confessio Amantis*, Vol. 1, edited by Russell A. Peck; with Latin translations by Andrew Galloway (2000); Vol. 2 (2003); Vol. 3 (2004)

Richard the Redeless and Mum and the Sothsegger, edited by James M. Dean (2000)

Ancrene Wisse, edited by Robert Hasenfratz (2000)

Walter Hilton, *The Scale of Perfection*, edited by Thomas H. Bestul (2000)

John Lydgate, *The Siege of Thebes*, edited by Robert R. Edwards (2001)

Pearl, edited by Sarah Stanbury (2001)

The Trials and Joys of Marriage, edited by Eve Salisbury (2002)

Middle English Legends of Women Saints, edited by Sherry L. Reames, with assistance of
   Martha G. Blalock and Wendy R. Larson (2003)
The Wallace: Selections, edited by Anne McKim (2003)
Richard Maidstone, *Concordia (The Reconciliation of Richard II with London)*, edited by
   David R. Carlson, with a verse translation by A. G. Rigg (2003)
Three Purgatory Poems: The Gast of Gy, Sir Owain, The Vision of Tundale, edited by Edward
   E. Foster (2004)
William Dunbar, *The Complete Works*, edited by John Conlee (2004)
Chaucerian Dream Visions and Complaints, edited by Dana M. Symons (2004)
Stanzaic Guy of Warwick, edited by Alison Wiggins (2004)
Saints' Lives in Middle English Collections, edited by E. Gordon Whatley, with Anne B.
   Thompson and Robert K. Upchurch (2004)
Siege of Jerusalem, edited by Michael Livingston (2004)
The Kingis Quair and Other Prison Poems, edited by Linne R. Mooney and Mary-Jo Arn
   (2005)
Chaucerian Apocrypha: Selections, edited by Kathleen Forni (2005)

DOCUMENTS OF PRACTICE SERIES

Love and Marriage in Late Medieval London, selected, translated, and introduced by
   Shannon McSheffrey (1995)
Sources for the History of Medicine in Late Medieval England, selected, introduced, and
   translated by Carole Rawcliffe (1995)
A Slice of Life: Selected Documents of Medieval English Peasant Experience, edited, translated,
   and with an introduction by Edwin Brezette DeWindt (1996)
Regular Life: Monastic, Canonical, and Mendicant Rules, selected and introduced by
   Douglas J. McMillan and Kathryn Smith Fladenmuller (1997); second edition,
   selected and introduced by Daniel Marcel La Corte and Douglas J. McMillan (2004)
Women and Monasticism in Medieval Europe: Sisters and Patrons of the Cistercian Reform,
   selected, translated, and with an introduction by Constance H. Berman (2002)
Medieval Notaries and Their Acts: The 1327–1328 Register of Jean Holanie, introduced,
   edited, and translated by Kathryn L. Reyerson and Debra A. Salata (2004)

COMMENTARY SERIES

Haimo of Auxerre, *Commentary on the Book of Jonah*, translated with an introduction and
   notes by Deborah Everhart (1993)
Medieval Exegesis in Translation: Commentaries on the Book of Ruth, translated with an intro-
   duction and notes by Lesley Smith (1996)
Nicholas of Lyra's Apocalypse Commentary, translated with an introduction and notes by
   Philip D. W. Krey (1997)
Rabbi Ezra Ben Solomon of Gerona, *Commentary on the Song of Songs and Other Kabbalistic
   Commentaries*, selected, translated, and annotated by Seth Brody (1999)
John Wyclif, *On the Truth of Holy Scripture*, translated with an introduction and notes by
   Ian Christopher Levy (2001)

Second Thessalonians: Two Early Medieval Apocalyptic Commentaries, introduced and translated by Steven R. Cartwright and Kevin L. Hughes (2001)

The Glossa Ordinaria *on the Song of Songs*, translated with an introduction and notes by Mary Dove (2004)

MEDIEVAL GERMAN TEXTS IN BILINGUAL EDITIONS SERIES

Sovereignty and Salvation in the Vernacular, 1050–1150, introduction, translations, and notes by James A. Schultz (2000)

Ava's New Testament Narratives: "When the Old Law Passed Away," introduction, translation, and notes by James A. Rushing, Jr. (2003)

History as Literature: German World Chronicles of the Thirteenth Century in Verse, introduction, translation, and notes by R. Graeme Dunphy (2003)

VARIA

The Study of Chivalry: Resources and Approaches, edited by Howell Chickering and Thomas H. Seiler (1988)

Studies in the Harly Manuscript: The Scribes, Contents, and Social Contexts of British Library MS Harley 2253, edited by Susanna Fein (2000)

The Liturgy of the Medieval Church, edited by Thomas J. Heffernan and E. Ann Matter (2001); second edition (2005)

TO ORDER PLEASE CONTACT:

Medieval Institute Publications
Western Michigan University
Kalamazoo, MI 49008-5432
Phone (269) 387-8755
FAX (269) 387-8750

http://www.wmich.edu/medieval/mip/index.html

Medieval Institute Publications is a program
of The Medieval Institute, College of Arts
and Sciences, Western Michigan University

Typeset in 10/13 New Baskerville
with Golden Cockerel Ornaments display
Designed by Linda K. Judy
Manufactured by _____

Medieval Institute Publications
College of Arts and Sciences
Western Michigan University
1903 W. Michigan Avenue
Kalamazoo, MI 49008-5432
http://www.wmich.edu/medieval/mip

 WESTERN MICHIGAN UNIVERSITY